W9-CCC-425

A YEAR OFF

A story about traveling
the world—and how to make it
happen for you

ALEXANDRA *and* DAVID BROWN

Library of Congress Cataloging-in-Publication Data

Names: Brown, Alexandra (Teacher), author. | Brown, David (Teacher), author.
Title: A year off / Alexandra and David Brown.
Description: San Francisco : Chronicle Books, 2018.
Identifiers: LCCN 2017030649 | ISBN 9781452164656 (hc : alk. paper)
Subjects: LCSH: Travel—Guidebooks.
Classification: LCC G153.4 .B76 2018 | DDC 910.4—dc23 LC record available
at https://lccn.loc.gov/2017030649

Manufactured in China

Design and illustrations by Jennifer Tolo Pierce
All photographs were taken by Alexandra and David Brown.

ExOfficio® is a registered trademark of Newell Brands.
Ziploc® is a registered trademark of SC Johnson.

Chronicle books and gifts are available at special quantity
discounts to corporations, professional associations, literacy
programs, and other organizations. For details and discount
information, please contact our corporate/premiums department
at corporatesales@chroniclebooks.com or at 1-800-759-0190.

10 9 8 7 6 5 4 3 2 1

Chronicle Books LLC
680 Second Street
San Francisco, California 94107
www.chroniclebooks.com

CONTENTS

SECTION I / BEFORE YOU GO / 13

CHAPTER 1 / TAKING THE FIRST STEP / 14

After dreaming about an adventure like this, the first step is deciding to actually go. From making the decision to quitting your job, this chapter provides advice on how to make your dream a reality and face the emotional responses you'll encounter not only from others but also from yourself.

CHAPTER 2 / PLANNING YOUR ROUTE / 50

Planning your general course is the first key component of your trip. This chapter offers a process for planning your overall route, including making a "must see" list and evaluating critical components that influence your route, like weather. An annotated map helps you see your route, as well as shows the route we took.

CHAPTER 3 / SETTING THE BUDGET / 70

Once your general route is set, it's much easier to finalize your budget. Suggested regional budgets and daily averages show you how to divide your funds across your journey. We also share the tricks we learned to help cut costs and maximize money and resources.

CHAPTER 4 / PREPPING AND PACKING / 92

You have a sense of your route, and you know your budget. Now you can begin to pack and prepare to depart. Our packing list shows you what you really need for the journey ahead, and we offer advice on the critical components to address before you leave. (Hint: fewer than you think!)

CHAPTER 9 / ADJUSTING TO REVERSE CULTURE SHOCK / 220

Coming home after being on the road for a long time can be shocking. This chapter offers advice on how to come home gracefully and prepare for the reverse culture shock that can hit harder than leaving did.

CHAPTER 10 / FINDING A NEW PERSPECTIVE ON YOUR OLD LIFE / 238

Once you come home, you may find the things you want have changed or, even more surprising, remained the same. We share our story from our first year back, offer perspective on the different ways a trip like this can affect how you move forward, and introduce questions to ask yourself upon your return to help you discover what you want now.

DEDICATION

This book is dedicated to all the wonderful people who helped give us a sense of home along the way: Aaron Swanton, Adham Abdullah, Alex Leonte, Antonio Soave, Barry Slaven, Cem Turan, Dan Chainer, Dan and Sarah Hess, Daniel Grier, Dominique Hess, Dorin Dumitriu, Elodie Vadala, Emilie Bannwarth, Franco Riva and Rosella Terzollo, Friederike Seybold, Gail Hammer, Gayle Brandt, Gary and Lauren Womack, Giuliano Morse, Howard "Buck" Hansen, Ignazio Marino, Jennie Aleshire Moctezuma, Josh Haftel, Jason Comer, Julien Sauve, Juz Cottoncity, Kelly Jones, Ken Carter, Kevin and Emily Couturier, Kim Riemer, Krystal Grossman-Smith, Lilian Debra Holzman, Manuela Bosch, Marian and Adriana Milut, Matthew Cervourst, Matt and Megan Lawson, Mav and Kane Georgeson, Meeta Bharvani, Michael and Jen Dezso, Monique Trouette, Nate Linkon, Nell and Jim Gleason, Nicki Christie, Noriaki and Ai Obata, Patty and Roland Hess, Peter Moennig, Pietro Condorelli, Rahul Kapur, Roli Arun, Saahil and Neha Goel, Shabari Padaki, Shekhar Deshpande, Simon Fessler, Soumya Tea, Sowmya and Hans Van Baaren, Stefano Salvadori, Tricia Puskar, and Vaunda and Drew Nelson . . . and, of course, our families.

INTRODUCTION

You can do this. Whether you are planning, daydreaming, or in the midst of deciding, the truth is that your trip has already begun.

So when does imagining metamorphose into action? This is not everyone's story, and nor do we expect it to be, but how and why we arrived at our desire to travel is not uncommon. Although we were both going through some big changes, there was nothing dreadfully amiss about our lives. We loved our friends and our home, and we had sound careers. Day-to-day life was good, but we were longing for something more fulfilling. We wanted to take a risk, living bigger than before and following our hearts, but we also felt fearful about stepping off the path of our traditional careers, eventual kids, and, down the road, retirement.

As people who love to travel, we also couldn't swallow the standard American corporate vacation philosophy, which often does not allow for enough time to actually travel. After holidays with family, there are usually just enough vacation days left to get somewhere, almost unwind to the point of being present, and then head home. It was amazing how often we heard people talking about how they were going to travel when they retired or wanted to travel now but didn't know how.

We found that existing books and guides did not touch on the benefits and challenges of taking a big journey during the stretch between settling into your career and retirement. In general, we found most were written for a college-aged backpacker or a vacationer with only a few days to spend. Many round-the-world books were written from a career wanderlust perspective, for people planning to leave and never come back.

Nothing was designed for people who have been working and enjoying a good life but who want to deeply experience the world while they are in that elusive sweet spot: young enough to enjoy it yet old enough to appreciate it. We could not find a book that possessed the voice of a friend who had walked this road before and could inspire us to dream of what we would want for our own journey, and how to return from it and reenter our lives smoothly.

Without a road map, we decided the best first step was to believe that *this* was possible.

We felt so many varying emotions, swinging from incredible feelings of appreciation and excitement to pangs of anxiety for what we "should" have been doing. Slowly over time, we learned to laugh in the face of our fears and redefine success based on our values, not our expectations. These attitude shifts proved to be our most valuable asset on the trip as well as in our lives after coming home. We want to encourage you to embrace your own process, as it is the key to receiving what may be the most impactful and amazing moments of your life.

We know that after years of establishing a life and career, the thought of veering off the path and pursuing another is exhilarating and terrifying. If you are feeling hesitation or fear about a trip, remember that everything you are leaving behind will most likely be there when you return, but the opportunity for an experience like this one may rapidly fade. If you are privileged enough to have the interest and means to take your trip of a lifetime, the actual big risk is the regret you may feel if you choose to not go in lieu of spending another year at work. We cannot urge you enough to invest now so you can benefit from the memories and perspective for the rest of your life.

We want to help you engage even more in the entire process of what you are about to do, from making the decision to go to coming home. On the course of our journey, we learned pretty quickly that traveling is not a vacation. Our own experiences, and those of others we've met who have done a similar thing, can offer a little perspective on navigating that difference. As with most worthwhile things in life, this process, from daydream to first ticket, was not always easy, stress-free, or even relaxing for us. Our hope is to impart some of the wisdom we gained through our collective experiences to help you define what you want; better manage the pre-, during-, and postplanning process; and engage deeply with the cultures and places you visit. In short, we wrote the book we wish we had read before we left, and we hope it helps you start your journey, even if it is just a daydream for now.

MEET THE AUTHORS

We had only known each other for a little over two months when we decided to quit our desk jobs and travel the world together for a year. It was and still is the most radical thing either of us has ever done. We were in love and knew it from the first date. It was in those first hours of conversation that our talk of round-the-world travel began.

David had been planning a solo trip to Europe and Japan, and as a bit of a joke we started imagining how we could live out this idea together: journeying with nothing but a few essentials, exploring all the places and people that captured David's imagination. But over the next few weeks we started craving something we could build together instead. With the help of our community, we began the work of clarifying what we wanted and purging ourselves of the "impossible" attitude. We realized fresh starts can begin every second and catering to fears would lead to a small and restricted existence. We put one foot in front of the other and set our hearts and minds to making the adventure possible.

In the end, we decided to expand the course of our trip and extend its duration, beginning in the United States and then going from east to west around the world. After only four months of dating, we hit the road and spent the next eleven months traveling the globe and getting to know each other in the process. Early into the trip, a friend sent us a clip of Bill Murray crashing a bachelor party where he said, "If you have someone who you think is the one, take that person and travel around the world. And go to places that are hard to go to and hard to get out of . . . When you come back, if you are still in love with that person, get married at the airport." In the backs of our minds, we had the same plan.

It was **THE BEST YEAR.**

We visited twenty countries over the course of one year. We reconnected with old friends all around the world and made countless connections with new ones. We saw, heard, tasted, and smelled so many different and beautiful things. We ate like locals and got food poisoning, more than once. The tastiness was well worth the discomfort. We drank an inordinate amount of coffee. We took thousands and thousands and thousands of photos. We rode in most every type of moving "vehicle" imaginable, including auto-rickshaws, scooters, canoes, kayaks, longboats, overnight sleeper buses, ferries, beds of pickup trucks, motor-cycles, planes, trains, and automobiles. We saw lots of the world. We saw even more of ourselves. And we learned how to see each other.

And, yes, when we got back, we did get married.

SECTION I

BEFORE YOU GO

Taking the First Step

THE FIRST STEP

David

Everyone's experience of taking the first major step is going to be different, as everyone has unique contexts and perspectives. At the time we decided to take our trip, Alexandra had lived in four cities over the previous year and was a freelancer. I, on the other hand, was quite rooted in San Francisco and in my career. No matter the circumstance, the choice to go is a significant decision.

From our experience, there is no simple path to follow when it comes to mustering the courage needed to deviate from the norm or *your* norm. Finding the kernel of personal truth that enables you to know this trip is the right decision is a deeply personal process. We each had unique processes of coming to terms with our decision once it was made, but we also found comfort and insight in the stories of others who had consciously deviated from more traditional paths, as well as from the people we were so afraid of disappointing with our decision to go.

While we thought the first step was deciding to go, in reality it was putting that decision into action: quitting our jobs, telling our families and friends, and grappling with the troupe of emotions that came barreling in once we turned our lives upside down. In this chapter, we offer tools and perspective on how to gracefully quit your job, tell the people in your life about your decision to travel, and approach the different emotional responses you may feel after making your decision.

15

How It All Began

San Francisco, CA

ALEXANDRA

37.7749° N, 122.4194° W

We were on what I thought was our first date but what David later claimed was just a "friendly hangout." Considering we worked together, this was a delicate dance. It was the first time we had hung out together as people, not as client and agency. Conversation felt effortless, and there was an invigorating crackle of electricity between us.

I had never felt more comfortable talking to a person I barely knew, and I felt this insane compulsion to reveal my heart and soul to him. David possessed this incredibly compelling combination of compassion, openness, understanding, and kindness. It was disarming and magnetic at the same time, and for the first time in my romantic life, I felt *seen*. His blue eyes revealed the inherent gentleness of his spirit and goodness of his heart. When he smiled, I couldn't help but immediately smile back. We were each caught up in the glorious sensation of being out with someone we genuinely liked. The evening was easy and magical. When David told me about his plan to quit his steady corporate job to spend three months traveling through Europe on a motorcycle and then visit Japan, I said the only thing that made sense in that moment:

"Wait for me."

The words hung between us in a thick silence. My spontaneous outburst shocked us both. The statement was ridiculous, but the gravity was not lost on either of us. Despite the objectively crazy nature of the suggestion, we could feel there was something real, something worth investigating, behind it. David paused.

"OK," he said. "I will."

The complete lack of filter on my part opened up a vulnerability and tenderness in our new relationship that never went away. After we said good night, I regretted not kissing David, and I sent him a short text saying as much. He later said it was this total lack of subtlety and "game" that endeared me to him. Soon after he said to a friend, "I'm pretty sure that was my last first date."

Things moved quickly after that. I quit my job at the agency where I worked in San Diego and became a freelancer so I could move up to San Francisco to be with David. I moved in with him under the pretense that it was just a temporary arrangement to save money—that is, if we didn't decide to travel together.

We had begun seriously talking about an extended international trip on the drive up from San Diego to San Francisco, daydreaming about the places we could go and how long we would take. We would lie in bed at night, excitedly talking about all the different possibilities and imagining what a life on the road together would look like. The conversations would reach a fever pitch, and then we would inevitably feel overwhelmed and decide it was all too soon, that we should stay in San Francisco and date "normally" for a while before doing anything dramatic.

But one night after we had been dating for a little over three weeks, it became very clear our intentions for each other were strong enough to consider embarking on an adventure together. We were talking about our most recent relationships and the things we had learned. David opened up about his past broken engagement, and I asked how he felt about marriage now. He said he still thought marriage was a good idea, assuming it's with the right kind of partner. As he spoke, I let myself be carried away by the soothing tone of his voice and the comfort of his honesty and genuine spirit. He spoke for a while before pausing and asking me, "Do you want to get married?" I felt my breath catch.

"OK," I answered.

"OK?" he responded with a bewildered expression.

Within seconds, I realized this was not a proposal. The heat of embarrassment flooded my body, and I hid under the covers in an attempt to disappear. I remember thinking, *Oh my god, I am such an idiot. This is the type of stuff guys run from.* I had no idea what he could be thinking. I was pretty sure he was in love with me too, although we had not yet crossed the "I love you" relationship hurdle.

And even then, saying "I love you" is a far cry away from "I want to marry you." Most guys would have placated me in the moment and then not called me back ever again, but David was different. He lifted the covers to look me straight in the eye and said, "You're adorable."

After that night, David's travel plans became our travel plans, and a three-month motorcycle trip through Europe became a one-year journey around the world. We had only known each other for two months when we officially made the decision to go, but that didn't matter as much as any reasonable person would assume. To a bystander, our decision must have looked like a recipe for disaster. To our friends and families, we were crazy fools in love who would, at least, get some interesting travel in while rapidly sorting our compatibility. Some people secretly placed bets about how long we would actually last once we left the country. Others were worried we could put too much pressure on top of a new relationship and ruin something great. *We knew it was risky for many reasons, but we trusted our guts and forged ahead, making plans to leave in a matter of months.*

In late August we decided we would officially hit the road just a few months later, on November 1. David had been saving for a shorter but more costly trip, so it seemed to us we could make those funds stretch the year. Assuming I could stay at David's apartment, finish my work contract, and sell my Honda Fit, I could also have enough by the fall. With what we had, we would be able to live comfortably yet modestly without working for a year and still have additional savings to live off of for six months when we got back home. Upon realizing this, we were both a bit shocked, but the trip we envisioned was not nearly as costly as we had expected.

Our planning cycle kept an accelerated clip similar to our relationship; we were a couple that dove in and moved fast, and our preparations for the trip were no different. We had two months to make a departure plan at work, wrap up loose ends at home, and take care of visas and vaccinations. The night before David and I gave our notices at work happened to be Rosh Hashanah, the Jewish New Year. Over a dinner of roast chicken with a friend, we each set some intentions for the year ahead, and the realization of what was about to happen hit us. The symbolism of the holiday sunk in for the first time. Our new year began that night.

Making It Real

San Francisco, CA

DAVID

37.7749° N, 122.4194° W

From the moment I awoke, I felt anxious and unfocused. I was going to quit my job in four hours. My fears and doubts were eating me alive, and I had to get them out in the open. Desperate for help, I took some advice from a friend to literally say everything in my head aloud, get it all out there, and see what held water. I went into my room, closed the door, and let it all out: *"David, who do you think you are? This is both irresponsible and foolish. No one will catch you if you fall. There is a solid chance this will ruin your professional reputation and you will pay for it for the rest of your career. You barely know this woman. This may ruin what seems like a totally incredible relationship. Travel will not solve anything."* The list went on and on.

Eventually, my mind quieted, and I felt more connected to my gut. In that moment of calm, the same belief that compelled me to want to do the trip in the first place came back to me: pursuing this adventure was the most honest step forward in my life. It was not perfect, but nothing ever is.

I finished my morning routines and left for work. Walking into the office that day I felt surprisingly clear on how I was going to spill the beans on this plan. I had a great professional relationship with my bosses. I felt especially indebted to my direct boss for all he had taught me over the past few years. I was unsure how either would respond, and was nervous about burning a bridge, but I felt they deserved to hear my honest and authentic story, not the corporate edit.

During our meetings, I expressed my gratitude for the incredible education and experience they had provided me. I put my decision to leave in the larger context of my past life and future goals. I shared with them the process that got me to this point and my desire to feel inspired again. I even revealed my feelings about the crazy and exhilarating new love in my life and the momentum it had created. I was also very candid about the fact that my heart was no longer in my role and how it pained me not to live up to a standard in which I could take pride. I can only imagine they were taken off guard by both the news and my candor.

I always knew my bosses cared for me beyond a professional level, but our conversations that day were so human. I had a strong sense they genuinely wanted the best for me. One boss even said, *"Well, pitching a new exciting role seems futile. I'm sad to lose you, but I'm excited to hear about what's to come."* Leaving these meetings, I felt a surprising sense of support. For weeks leading up to giving notice, I had imagined leaving the office and feeling a combination of freedom, fear, and finality. I was abandoning the protection of my well-defined career and deserting what I had worked so hard to achieve, along with those who had invested so much in helping me do so. Those emotions were part of it, but I also felt excitement, understanding, and encouragement. I did not *need* their permission, nor was I requesting anything from them, but they chose to wish me the very best and offered to help me if I ever needed it. I believed they would. They had given me their blessings.

HOW TO PREPARE FOR AND HAVE "THE TALK" WITH YOUR BOSS

Deciding to quit your job to travel the world can feel like an enormous step, but actually telling the people you work with can feel equally big in its own way. How you approach the conversation will ultimately depend on what you may want after you come back, but there are a few steps to consider in making the whole process more fruitful for everyone.

1/ Reconsider the "guns blazing" approach that you may be fantasizing about. You never know what the future holds and what you may want in a year. If you need some catharsis, do a little role-playing with friends over drinks so you can really give it to the man, but be respectful when it comes time for the actual talk.

2/ To be honest with your boss, start by being honest with yourself and getting clear on your intentions. Before the talk, make a list broken out in sections: the reasons you want to take this trip, what you're hoping to get from travel, how long you are considering being away, and how you feel about returning to your career or even your current company if that's an option.

continued ←•

3/ Take the opportunity to see your boss as a person and invite him or her to share in your experience, which will help him or her realize that this is a personal investment, not just a "year-long vacation." Gauge how much you want to share depending on your relationship and your boss's personality, but even if you do not have a deep connection, piquing your boss's interest in your journey may make staying in touch after you go much more natural and likely.

4/ Put together a work plan for your departure. Let your current employer know how you intend to make the transition as smooth as possible. Although this is extra work you technically do not need to do, it can go a long way in preserving the relationship and making you feel good about your departure.

LETTING GO OF EXPECTATIONS

Alexandra

While the conversations with our bosses went well, the conversations with our families were more nuanced. We were reminded that parents stay parents even when you're in your thirties, and parents worry. David's parents did not question his decision, as they were more adjusted to his free-spirited approach to life and trusted his track record of having always somehow landed solidly on his feet, but the idea of us being in India for six weeks scared them. My parents wanted a lot of answers. They had always been proud of my academic achievements and career choices, so seeing me step off the familiar path unsettled them. They didn't express confidence that I could do the trip. I had also developed a reputation in the family for being impulsive and quick to bail when things didn't turn out as expected, and this trip made it clear that that shadow remained. These conversations made me question if I was really doing it for myself or to prove something to everyone else.

The questions and concerns rattled us, and a voice of judgment inside would whisper, *"You have no idea what you are doing!"* Yet as the weeks went on, we grew more and more comfortable with our choice and were able to slowly let go of the expectations that we imagined others had for us but that were really coming from within. We started seeing opportunities to invite people into the dialogue of how we got where we were, and the more we opened up, the more inspiring their responses became. More often than not, when we told somebody about what we were doing, they would start sharing their dreams and reveal deeply personal information about the choices, good and bad, they had made in their lives. It was amazingly reassuring.

THE OPINIONS OF OTHERS

You're going to be eager to tell your family, friends, colleagues, and the person you just met in line at the grocery store about your travel plans, and people are going to be eager to share their opinions about your travel plans with you. The truth is that most people will be excited to hear some details of your plans and even inspired to do something similar. On the whole, responses will likely range from support to quiet reservation to blatant judgment. Someone is bound to say, "Well, aren't you lucky." Which is true, but his or her intention may not be to inspire a great feeling of gratitude about all the privileges that come with being middle-class or above in the U.S. There is also a good chance someone in your family or inner circle will experience great fear for your safety and suggest you get a GPS tracking device or at minimum provide you with a heart-felt talking-to about the dangers of places outside the U.S.

Then there's jealousy, which can come from anywhere. One of our favorite digs we like to repeat to each other periodically was from someone who could have easily afforded our trip several times over. He said, "Oh, wow, a yearlong vacation during a down economy. That must be nice." We did not respond.

Random strangers may even have an opinion or two to share on the topic. Cocktail party conversation can quickly devolve into an analysis of your future journey with eager and unwanted assessments of your proposed path and attitudes on polariz-ing countries like India. One way or another, people are going to have opinions.

continued ←--→

TIP 1: ▶ What someone else thinks isn't a reflection of you or the choice you've made. For those who feel they have earned or were bestowed with superior logic and a handle on all truth, feel free to toss out or say to yourself, "You be you; I'll handle being me."

TIP 2: ▶ Be aware that your actions can translate into statements. You are rocking the boat on several levels and taking advantage of privilege. No matter how scary or challenging taking this step may be, it is a luxury. Although there are many people who want to take a trip like this, most are not in the position to do so. Be sensitive when talking about your upcoming travel plans or sharing updates from abroad, and don't get defensive if someone makes an offhand remark about your trip. Leaving for such a long period of time may also cause the people closest to you to feel abandoned. Stay focused on what you are doing while thoughtfully affirming the positions they have in your life.

TIP 3: ▶ The reactions of family and close friends may hold the most weight for you. If the feedback is less than positive, it is well worth listening to their perspective, but remember that their perspective is just that: theirs, not yours. They may have a myriad of reasons for challenging your decision, many of them likely well-intentioned, but their opinions are inherently products of their context and life view. For example, no matter your age, parents may express concern for your safety, career, or any number of things, but we found it best to just see this as an expression of love rather than disapproval. Friends may express some disappointment, yet this is likely to be more about missing you or feeling abandoned than about criticizing your trip. Including your family and close friends in your process can help alleviate some of the potential tension, but if it doesn't, take a step back to avoid unnecessary conflict.

PUSHING OFF

After quitting our jobs and telling our families and friends of our plans, we moved forward knowing we could not turn back to what we had had. This visceral understanding incited action. We dove deeper into making a list of all the things we thought we needed to take care of before we left and read anything we could get our hands on or find on the internet. The next two months flew by at a breathless pace, but we were somehow able to stay thoughtful with our time. Perhaps it was because we knew our days left in San Francisco were limited, or maybe it was the renewed sense of energy we felt after giving notice at work. Either way, those weeks were full and vibrant. On November 1, we took off on our Great American Road Trip, a two-month journey traveling along the perimeter of the country visiting family and friends, with a two-week interlude in Costa Rica to pressure test our travel gear in an international setting. We still had a lot of planning and prepping to do, most of which we'd decided to tackle while on the road trip, but technically our trip had begun.

Reaching the Badlands

South Dakota

DAVID

43.8554° N, 102.3397° W

Exhausted, sore, and hungry; it was painfully obvious I was no longer eighteen years old. For the last five days, my six-foot-three body had been packed in a tiny car. The sadist who designed the interior of the Honda Fit must have taken some sinister pleasure in the irony of its name. We were a week out from our last days in the office and at the beginning of our self-inflicted race across the U.S.

We had pulled over somewhere in South Dakota and were trying to find something to eat. For the past few hours, my mind had rested in the familiar comfort of dreaming about great food—specifically about what new and interesting food we could find that night. I imagined us discovering some hot spot in town serving the local favorites. Maybe venison sausage with some Sioux Tribe–inspired cornmeal breads and a local beer. Alexandra has celiac disease, which makes eating out tricky to say the least, but with some explaining, it's usually doable.

After clear over an hour of visiting every establishment having anything to do with food in a twenty-mile radius, my stomach had taken full control of my brain. It was taking all my focus and energy to contain my inner whiny child. We needed to take what we could get, and I needed to get out of the car before I started to let my feelings show. I suddenly saw the Domino's we had passed several times in our search in a new light. As we got closer, we spotted an ad pasted in the window: *Now Serving Gluten-Free Pizza!* I felt both repulsed and relieved. Alexandra ordered the pizza while I made a poor choice with the pasta carbonara. The disinterested employee tossed a frozen gluten-free pizza in the oven and began to work on my pasta. I was mesmerized as he proceeded to pound a squeeze bottle against the counter, squirted thick white sauce onto noodles in a plastic container, and then flipped the whole thing in a microwave oven.

I quit my career for this. The sentence rang in my head as if some punk kid whispered it in my ear while passing. My hungry-stomach brain couldn't dismiss the statement's relevance in my current situation. I was not having fun, my exhaustion was debilitating, my days lacked identifiable value, I felt completely goalless, and I was burning through my savings. And for what exactly?

It was finally time for bed, but despite my exhaustion, I could barely sleep. Maybe it was because our Airbnb was in a massive building I suspected was a Y2K compound and later repurposed as an Evangelical church's retreat center . . . or maybe it was the carbonara. It was most likely due to the fact I felt completely rudderless and overwhelmed with anxiety about my future. Did I just trade a successful career and an awesome life in San Francisco to become a directionless vagabond? I was questioning if this was a bold step toward owning my life and decisions or if I was just a burnout. In the years before the trip I slept very little, trying to squeeze in an overloaded social schedule and a very demanding job. I dedicated far too many hours to my office life, took too few vacations, and was not sure if I even valued what I did. Maybe all my woo-woo philosophizing was really only my justifying running from my fucked-up life.

The next day was another long day of driving. I tried to be a pleasant travel partner while I toiled internally. Alexandra was concerned about me, but I wasn't yet ready to share. My thoughts felt totally unclear, and I was far too embarrassed to even reveal the theme. We eventually arrived at Badlands National Park. It was beautiful, but I still couldn't break out of the funk. A light dusting of snow on the ground reflected the golden colors of the sun as it approached the horizon. As we arrived at an intersection, we came upon a bighorn sheep that had walked onto the road. We stopped the car. I expected it to run away, but it remained. We got out of the car and looked down the hill to discover a herd of forty or more bighorn sheep. We quickly realized they were all about to cross in front of us, so we grabbed our coats and stood in the middle of the empty road waiting.

The sheep were surprisingly tranquil, and many of them made eye contact with us. It felt as though they were assessing our intentions for being there. I was captivated, and my mind went silent. The

cold air froze my nostrils, and my eyes watered from the occasional frigid gusts interrupting the otherwise perfect stillness. I felt inexplicably calm. The animals passed one by one. Some were massive while others were smaller than deer. A young sheep came up right next to me and gave me a trusting look, then walked to Alexandra and stood by her side. They stood on the edge of the road together and overlooked the migration below. I was in complete awe. My body buzzed with light as I stared at Alexandra and the young sheep watching the sunset like old friends. *Something began to crack inside me.* **I am here for a reason,** *I heard a bold voice say.* I could choose to see my situation otherwise, but then I'd miss the beauty of it all. This moment was not my goal nor part of the plan, but it was perfect. This was why we were here. It was why we were doing this.

WHAT HAVE I DONE?

Alexandra

Those first few weeks on the road shone a light on how much pride David and I had taken in having long been on a course of "doing the right thing." We had spent our mid- to late-twenties working hard at jobs that held clout and earning our reputations in our respective fields. David had put himself through college as well as an MBA program. The MBA was indicative of his choice to abandon the artist lifestyle he, his parents, and his friends were a part of in order to establish what he considered a more stable and "normal" life. I had diligently followed the high-achiever track, going from prep school to a top university to a fast-paced job in advertising. Throughout our twenties, we both worked to amass achievements that fit what most Americans deemed as "success," but no promotion, milestone, or praise we had received thus far gave us a sincere feeling of accomplishment.

The trip felt like a solution to this, but departing from the world we had known was still jarring. We were taken aback by how much anxiety leaving our jobs and a steady paycheck triggered in us, and we weathered a lot of emotional ups and downs. During the hours we spent in the car on the way to our first stop, David's grandfather's home in Wisconsin, we would talk and talk and talk about everything we hoped to do with our newfound freedom and sure-to-follow unbridled creativity.

41

We spoke about learning how to play all the songs on Bon Iver's *For Emma, Forever Ago*. We committed to doing something physical every single morning. We thought we would even start writing a novel.

But what ended up happening once we got to Wisconsin was a lot of eating, sitting in front of the fire questioning what we were doing, and getting buzzed while watching old Jacques Cousteau films that a relative had left in the cabin years ago. We were freaked out, and the additional pressure we had applied to ourselves to do something completely amazing right from the start didn't help matters at all.

We had the hardest time with how to answer the question "what do you do?" now that we didn't have our old jobs. We suddenly found ourselves without the security blanket of a clear, concise title. In the U.S., what people do is often synonymous with who they are, and we felt at a loss for an answer. When we first left on our trip and people would ask us about what we did, we felt pressure to answer briefly but would end up rambling, over explaining our decision and ultimately coming across as insecure. We simply didn't know how to respond. Were we travelers? Adventurers? Wanderers? The answer was unclear, and all the obvious choices lacked the depth we wanted to express about our journey.

Over the coming weeks, the voices of doubt would continue to creep into our thoughts, but they became easier to shake off. Embracing what we were doing fully became the only real option. We could no longer keep one foot in the door and one foot out. While it took leaving the country to really solidify our transition from working life to traveling life, the road trip and prepping period proved to be a testing ground for learning how to face our fears and begin accepting who we were.

EMOTIONAL SITUATIONS TO EXPECT

So much emotion can be wrapped up in making the decision to go that you expect to feel awash in an unbelievable sense of relief about everything thereafter, but the first chapter of the journey is rife with mixed feelings. Big change incites reaction; do not be surprised if you encounter one, if not all, of the following.

1/ Identity Crisis

If you are part of the nine-to-five working world or have any regularity within your day to day, there is a good chance that obliterating your way of life will throw you for an emotional loop. It seems obvious, but many people do not expect to have a strong reaction to this sort of change. From our experience and those of people we met on our travels, the intensity of the reaction seems directly related to three factors:

- Whether you are planning on returning to the same profession and life you had before you left or not.

- Whether your choice to take the trip was encouraged or discouraged by those around you.

- Whether you are able to afford to retain the luxuries in your current lifestyle or had to let those things go.

Depending on your answers to the above, you may feel slightly off every now and then, or you may find yourself questioning your very existence. You may regularly face questions like, "What the hell am I doing with my life?" or

"Who am I turning into?" On the other hand, you may find yourself saying, "I always thought I needed espresso to start my day, but now I am really enjoying tea. . . . I never thought *that* would happen." Wherever it falls on the spectrum of intensity, an identity crisis is a perfectly normal reaction to have when a big change takes place.

TIP: ▶ Take the time to write down your feelings. Doing this can be hard, irritating, and inconvenient, but you may gain some much-needed perspective. Most likely many of the thoughts you are having will sound a bit far-fetched once you read them, especially if you read them aloud. A lack of certainty around who you are and what you are about doesn't mean going on the trip is the wrong choice. It most likely means this trip is a brilliant idea and great things are in store for you. Make a list of these feelings, take a deep breath, and engage.

2/ Financial Freak-Outs

Spending money when you have a steady stream of income going into your bank account feels just fine. Spending money when you have nothing coming into your bank account can feel just awful. If you are accustomed to supporting yourself, not making money can be terrifying and lead to unneeded stress and anxiety. When money feels scarce, you may find yourself harshly evaluating how you spend your time, being excessively thrifty, or feeling stress every time you want to buy something. Fortunately, what you may discover is that the money tends to work out. Everyone we talked to ended

continued ▸⟶

up spending exactly what they thought they would when they left, ourselves included. Life on the road isn't nearly as expensive as you would imagine it to be, and you'll likely be surprised at how far your money can go.

TIP 1: ▶ When you are feeling stressed about money, remind yourself you are not on this trip to save money; you are here to enjoy.

TIP 2: ▶ Remind yourself that you can always go home early. Better to have amazing memories of all you experienced than to be able to say you went everywhere and experienced nothing.

TIP 3: ▶ Set aside a separate fund for luxuries and trinkets. If you have a stash for extraordinary experiences or expensive things you must buy and send home, you won't feel like you're losing a grip on your broader budget.

3/ Waves of Overwhelming Paralysis

When you suddenly find yourself with all the time in the world, you may have no idea what to do and end up watching hours of Netflix instead of reading that book on Buddhist philosophy you've been meaning to read but didn't have time to read because you were working, but now you're not working. . . . *What am I doing with my time?* Sometimes the luxury of having more time can result in a panic of feeling pressure to make the absolute most of that time. In moments like this, the waves of panic roll in and nothing feels satisfying.

TIP 1: ▶ Do not underestimate the power of a solid nap or a good night's sleep.

TIP 2: ▶ You have made the decision to take off because you want to invest your time and energy into something you care about. Do not abandon yourself. Keep up a positive attitude and drop any expectations, even if they seem valuable to you. They will limit you from getting a deeper and more intuitive understanding of yourself and those around you.

TIP 3: ▶ Take at least three deep breaths and ask yourself, "What would make my heart sing right now?" Yeah, we know, that sounds pretty ridiculous, and admittedly, it became a bit of a joke with us, but it works. Something about the silliness of the prompt can help you get out of your head for a second and take a moment to really consider how you want to spend your time. Don't fixate on what you "should" be doing or what you "need" to do. Instead, frame the decision by considering what will bring you the most joy in that moment. The sooner you learn how to give yourself what you want or need, the sooner this feeling will pass.

4/ Unbridled Joy

This one needs no explanation. Just savor it!

WAKE UP TO YOUR PRESENT

A good friend who is a well-seasoned traveler himself once told us travel is part fun, part self-discovery, and part hard work. We found the same goes for taking the first step toward embarking upon your trip. Bailing on the well-worn established path puts far more pressure on you to lead your own life and involves varying degrees of self-discovery. This is all to say that like any transition, there are lots of things that do not feel so great at first but may end up being pretty amazing in the end.

We learned not to set the expectations for our newfound freedom unreasonably high. We gave ourselves time to settle into seismic changes and made room for the numerous emotions that bubbled up. Looking back, that first flush of the trip was a time we will never forget. It was full of excitement and fear, adventure and doubt, letting go and holding on. It was an invitation to be present—an invitation that endured throughout the trip—and the first real opportunity to embrace who we wanted to be. It was a time to savor because it was a time we had only once, and the bigger journey was just ahead, eagerly waiting for us.

CHAPTER 2

Planning Your Route

🚲

There are countless different ways to spend a year traveling. Visit every continent, focus on one hemisphere or the other, crisscross the equator, or stay east versus west. There is no right or wrong route, but there are lots of factors to consider. In this chapter, we will offer tools to help you envision what you want from this trip, prioritize potential destinations, and ultimately create a route that will set you up for an amazing adventure.

We fell hard for the romance and ring of an "around the world" trip, so that became our foundation. Although we had a good start, we were far from having a route even when we set off on our Great American Road Trip. We were overwhelmed by possibility. We took a leap of faith and bought our first series of one-way tickets: New Zealand, Australia, Singapore, and Cambodia. It felt like a good start based on weather, interests, and people to visit. On the road, choices became easier as we began to learn more about decision-making from others and ourselves.

At the beginning, a year of traveling felt like a massive amount of time. We bought a foldout map of the world and would spend evenings chatting about the seemingly endless list of incredible places we could explore: Patagonia, South Africa, Kenya, Ethiopia, Japan, Thailand, Vietnam, India, Czech Republic, Scotland, France, Italy . . . the list went on and on. We wanted to experience it all. Every time we would learn more about a region or country, the more enticed we would become. Countries that only seemed vaguely interesting at first would start to become "must sees" as we learned more about their unique landscapes, food, traditions, and people.

Alongside our continuously growing list, a conflicting interest was gaining great strength. We did not want to only *see* places; we wanted to *experience* them. Experiencing the day-to-day nuances of a place and its people was what tour books and photos could not convey. We wanted to get to know locals, fall into the rhythm of real neighborhoods, and catch a glimpse of what it would be like to live there. To understand a place well enough to laugh at a native joke, throw out a bit of slang, and see the places locals loved even if they were not magnificent enough to make the tour books and blogs, these were things a trip like this could provide that a vacation could not.

As our desire to go to as many places as possible converged with an equally strong aspiration to deeply experience those same places, a year felt shockingly short, and planning and setting priorities became even more important.

51

A Recipe for Conflict

Pittsburgh, PA

ALEXANDRA

40.4406° N, 79.9959° W

David and I are both list makers. Lists feel like the calm in the storm by giving us focus and making the amorphous more defined. It was only natural that when we felt completely overwhelmed by the endless possibilities for our year of travel we would make a gigantic list and go from there. We started big, highlighting countries of particular interest, then got more specific, writing down sights, experiences, and cultural moments we didn't want to miss. As we added to our collective list, we found we not only had a lot of overlap between our wishes but also had one significant thing in common: we were both more interested in immersing ourselves in a specific place or culture than seeing a selection of sights. Making the list was easy and exhilarating, but cutting it was not.

Queue our first major fight.

We were about halfway through our road trip and five weeks away from leaving the country, and it was the week before Thanksgiving. We were visiting David's parents in Pittsburgh before heading to Atlanta to spend the holiday with my family. While driving back from meeting some of David's friends, we had gotten on the topic of time allocation in different regions during the international stage of our journey. Our opinions started to diverge, making room for our personality differences to take center stage. An anthropologist at heart, David leaned toward his instinct to go to the unfamiliar. Although he wanted to experience Europe, his desire to experience Southeast Asia, India, Africa, and South America began to take precedence. He saw Europe as a destination we could go back to again and again when we were older and had different travel preferences, particularly after having kids. I, on the other hand, was pushing for more of a balance. I felt the need to complement the periods of greater culture shock and potential discomfort with more familiar and comforting places. I also felt the pressure to make more "realistic" decisions based on our time constraints. Africa and South America sounded great, but would we actually have the time to do everything without spreading ourselves too thin?

The more we expressed our opinions, the more our emotions escalated until David pulled the car over into a parking lot near his parents' house. Although the conversation was focused on the route, it also grew out of the fact that we were very different people in many ways, especially when it came to danger, risks, and planning. I consider it wise to avoid danger, tend to gravitate to the familiar, and hold tightly to a plan, while David sees danger as part of doing great things, is curious about the unknown, likes to push his limits, and is likely to blow up the plan in hopes of building a better one.

Sitting in the car that night, these differences seemed insurmountable. I could feel David polarizing himself to me, and I felt forced into expressing the fears I preferred to manage internally. I wanted to scream, *"I am not an adventurer! You found me out!"* and I might have in the heat of the moment. I was scared of the unknown and hated how so much of this new lifestyle felt out of my control, yet despite all my fears and discomforts, I wanted this. I did not want to sacrifice the chance to embark on this incredible adventure with an amazing person because I was fearful. I knew I wasn't an adventurer at my core, and that my impulse to control everything would continue to be a near-constant struggle, but I wanted this adventure badly.

In that moment, the route discussion became the avenue for all my anxieties to come to the surface. I began to cry. I was terrified all of this would be a failure. David would not feel the same way for me as I did for him. I might have ruined my career. Our trip would end before we even left the country, and I was kidding myself to think I could handle doing something like this. In that moment, my heart was filled with fear as I envisioned what failure would mean for me. I had never put so much on the line.

Although I could feel that David knew my reaction was about more than just the route, the conversation never deviated. Eventually, we had nothing more to express. We sat in silence, and I could feel David drawing close to me again. My mind slowly stopped whirling.

David and I are more similar than either of us realized when it comes to how we approach life. He's not the cool, laid-back adventurer, artist type who flows with whatever, even if he sometimes comes off that way. He's very responsible, thoughtful, and dedicated. He's a long-term planner, a creature of habit, and far from graceful when it comes to change. He has quirky ways of ritualizing daily living, and these rituals make me feel grounded even with all the insanity we bring to our life together. He has systems for nearly everything, and I love them.

While all we could see in that moment were our differences, we knew we had more in common than not.

FINDING MIDDLE GROUND

If you plan to travel with someone, conflicting points of view are likely to arise. The obvious truth is that you can't change your personality, but you can adjust your approach to make it easier to plan a trip with a partner. We managed to address the route issue and recognized our list was simply too long for the amount of time and money we had. Every choice would also involve a sacrifice. We simply couldn't see and experience everything we wanted to see and do in one year. We went back through the list and approached each place with the question, *"Does the idea of going to this place fill you with tangible excitement?"* Over the next few weeks, we looked realistically at our list, the map, and how much money we had and made some difficult decisions. We recognized we had to hold on to seeing the things we wanted to see but let go of the need to see *everything*. We also let go of mapping out our entire route. We decided to adjust as we went. We finally felt free.

In the end, we have questioned many parts about the way we traveled, but our route was never one of them. This is not to say our route was perfect, but we couldn't have asked for something better. The list we ended with wasn't the list we had when we started, and many of the places we didn't get to see still hold the intrigue they did when we left, but we feel hopeful that someday we'll see those places too.

MAPPING YOUR ROUTE

With the exhilaration of so much open time and space before you, it's easy to get caught up and try to fit in everything you've always wanted to do. Realistically, this probably can't happen on one single trip, not unless you're gone for many, many years, so you make a plan. There are lots of factors to consider when figuring out what to see when. Some people will want to plan everything in advance. Others may not want to plan beyond the departure date and first ticket. Our own research and experience, combined with conversations we had with other travelers, helped us create a process that highlights key considerations for route planning. Our hope is that by addressing each element, you will be equipped to make wise decisions and have an easier time painting a picture of what your route may look like.

1/ List Destinations

Use a map and list every place you would love to visit. Do not overthink the first pass. Once you have a list, use these criteria to focus in on your must-visit locations and figure out what places you can let go of:

- ❋ What places excite you right now? Most likely you will have places you wanted to visit years ago but spark less interest now. If you focus on what you presently want, it will help you be even more excited about not only the trip but also the time spent researching. It should also help narrow your list.

continued ⟶

- ◎ Once you have a sense of the places that excite you, identify your top three destinations. What do you think you will regret not seeing? If we had done this before we left, Japan would have made our list, but we were too focused on budget and an efficient route. We did, however, adjust our plans once in Asia and made it to Japan, and it was definitely worth the effort!

- ☺ Next, mark where you have friends or family you could either stay with or who would be willing to show you around. Be liberal. This is a great time to reconnect with people even if you have not spoken in years, and having a local show you a place is invaluable!

- 🚫 Finally, mark places that may be better reserved for a future vacation. You will have more time on this trip, so this is the opportunity to really dig into a place if that is what you are craving.

- 💲 We will dive deeper into budget in our next chapter, but you may want to consider ranking your list by high-, medium-, and low-burn countries. In other words, what countries will burn through your budget faster? For example, we lived comfortably for a week in Darjeeling on what we spent in a night in London.

Once you have your filtered list, plot every destination on a world map. This will give you a sense of where everything is and whether the distances are manageable given your budget and timeline. After seeing where everything falls, you may notice patterns or a natural route taking shape. Depending on where things lie on the map, this will help form the basis of the overall direction you take.

2/ Start Thinking About the Direction of Your Route.
Having a list of destinations is a start, but there are a few important factors to consider when deciding what order to visit them in:

- **The *Five* Seasons:** We chose to chase summer for most of our trip with some spring and fall mixed in. We highly recommend this, as it enabled us to have longer, sunnier days, little rain, and lighter packs due to the lack of winter clothes. We were also careful to avoid places where the summer heat was unbearable. Another season we kept top of mind was monsoon/typhoon/rainy season. Being in Europe for rainy season is tolerable and even recommended if you are a foodie because of the fall harvest, but rainy season can mean something else entirely in other parts of the world. This isn't to say you can't visit India during monsoon season, but be prepared for near-constant rain, major travel delays, and more dangerous circumstances.

continued •—→

- **Cultural Adjustments:** Although extreme culture shock can be interesting to experience once or twice, it is draining. At best, it slows the process of understanding the place you are in and getting into the flow. At worst, it causes you to hate where you are and may necessitate a vacation from your trip. As a result, we highly recommend reducing it as much as possible. Factors such as economy, cleanliness, religious practices/restrictions, personal space, human rights, social norms, friendliness, and sense of order are well worth considering when planning your route. We consciously tried to "warm up" to unfamiliar or radically different cultural influences throughout our trip by gradually moving to countries that felt less and less familiar and reversing the process on the second half of our trip. Taking advantage of the fact that regions often have a significant amount of cultural diffusion, we moved slowly across the globe to help ease into a place while also being more efficient with our money. Although geography is a good general rule, it is far from infallible, so do your cultural research; it is fun and enriching anyway!

- **Peak Tourist Seasons:** In addition to weather seasons, there are tourist seasons. The two often go hand in hand, as most tourists visit a place during times of optimal weather. This is a potential downside of following the sun, as you could end up in a place when it's completely overrun with tourists, meaning costs are higher, accommodations are booked, transit is overloaded, and locals are frustrated and less likely to engage with you. On the other hand, visiting a place during the off-season often means poorer weather and fewer places open. It can be challenging to be strategic and still experience good weather without all the tourists, but one way to do this is to take advantage of fringe seasons. Right before or after the big rush is normally perfect. You may suffer an extra rainy day or two, but it is well worth it. Although tourists can make a place feel like an amusement park, they're not all bad. Certain places come alive with a crowd, particularly festivals, beach life, and cultural events. When it comes to tourists, the rule of thumb is to know when you want them.

MAPPING YOUR ROUTE

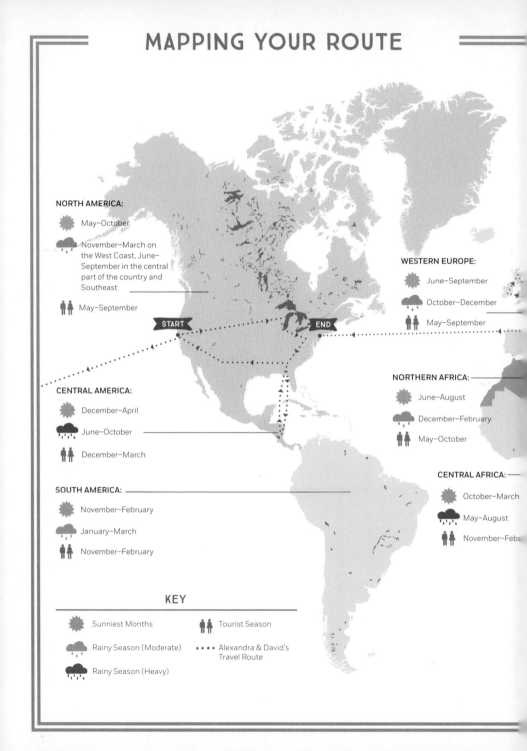

NORTH AMERICA:

May–October

November–March on the West Coast, June–September in the central part of the country and Southeast

May–September

CENTRAL AMERICA:

December–April

June–October

December–March

SOUTH AMERICA:

November–February

January–March

November–February

WESTERN EUROPE:

June–September

October–December

May–September

NORTHERN AFRICA:

June–August

December–February

May–October

CENTRAL AFRICA:

October–March

May–August

November–Febr

START

END

KEY

Sunniest Months

Tourist Season

Rainy Season (Moderate)

Alexandra & David's Travel Route

Rainy Season (Heavy)

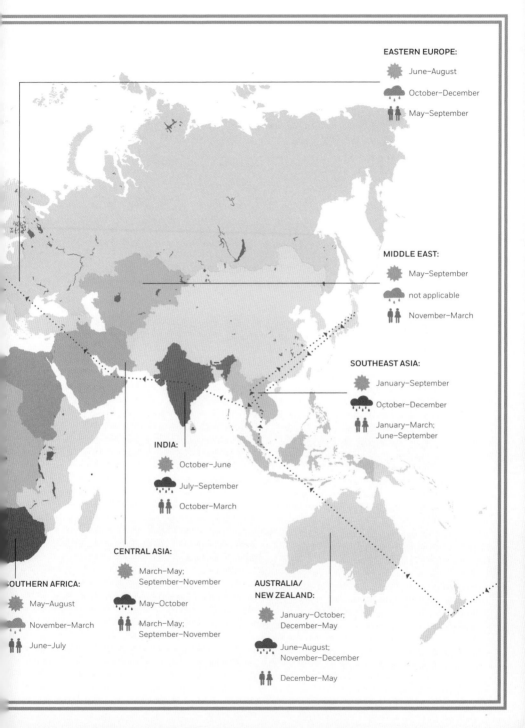

EASTERN EUROPE:
- June–August
- October–December
- May–September

MIDDLE EAST:
- May–September
- not applicable
- November–March

SOUTHEAST ASIA:
- January–September
- October–December
- January–March; June–September

INDIA:
- October–June
- July–September
- October–March

CENTRAL ASIA:
- March–May; September–November
- May–October
- March–May; September–November

AUSTRALIA/ NEW ZEALAND:
- January–October; December–May
- June–August; November–December
- December–May

SOUTHERN AFRICA:
- May–August
- November–March
- June–July

BRINGING IT ALL TOGETHER

One thing to keep in mind while planning your route is that nothing is final. The only thing really set is your start date. This type of trip is an iterative process, and your route will evolve as you travel. As we'll explain more in the next chapter, a lot of your transportation, including flights, can be booked on the fly, opening you up to so much more flexibility. In the end, places not on your list may end up being some of your favorites, and your top destinations may not be everything you hoped they would be.

Once you have your departure date, take a look at your map and see where you want to go first. A fantastic first destination would be one where the culture is not shockingly different from your own, as you may have your hands full transitioning into the travel life, and should be a place on your "must see" list with good weather and possibly a friend or two to build excitement. You will probably be able to handle the tourists better in the beginning of your trip versus the end, so do not worry as much about that.

After you have chosen your first stop, you can try out several possible routes from there. As you consider routes, challenge them against where they are in your list and how they fit in with the timing considerations of weather, culture shock, and tourist crowding. You will likely find it less painful to plan if you take things one step at a time and remember you can change it all up at any moment.

WHY WE LOVED OUR ROUTE

When we talk to other people interested in doing an extended trip, many of them ask whether we have a recommended route. The simple answer is no. Every person is different, and every trip is different. We absolutely loved our route and felt like it was perfect, but we've heard of other people really enjoying routes drastically different from the one we took. Our route was an east-to-west one, partly because we started in California but also for reasons connected to seasonality and climate, cultural transitions, and budget.

In addition to the good weather we had for most of our journey, we were able to catch some elusive seasonal moments that only happen once a year: cherry blossoms in Japan, harvest in Northern Italy, the Willie Clancy Festival in Ireland, and a water-logged New Year's in Thailand.

Another benefit to the direction we took was meeting European travelers while traveling in Asia who later invited us to join them in their home countries once we got to Europe. This expanded our network of friendly faces, offered us more-immersive visits from a local's perspective, and helped offset the cost of traveling in Europe tremendously.

But our favorite part of our route was the way we naturally managed the ebb and flow of culture shock. We intentionally began our trip in New Zealand—a destination that felt completely far away but with a context very familiar to life back home. We then eased our way into Southeast Asia by starting in Singapore before moving up into Cambodia, Laos, and Thailand. We bookended our interlude in Japan with Thailand so as not to make the transition into India as jolting. When we got to India, we had spent enough time in Southeast Asia to feel more at home in a frenetic, hectic, and crowded environment. On the other side, we knew going from India straight to Western Europe could have been too much of a shock for our systems, so we transitioned into Europe by starting in the east before moving to the west. By ending our trip in Western Europe, we also felt more prepared to come back home to the U.S. Throughout the trip, we did experience mild culture shock at times, but generally, our transitions were smooth and often exhilarating.

For as much time as we've thought about it, we've never questioned our route. In the end, we have no regrets on the direction we chose and the places we went. There are plenty of optimizations we could have made. We often talk about how we wish we had worried about money less or hadn't rushed in some places, and we really wish we hadn't let the anxieties about coming home occupy so much of our time and energy while still on the road. Yet when it came to the route itself, we were nothing but happy with our decisions.

CHAPTER 3

Setting the Budget

When you tell people you are taking a yearlong trip around the world, the first question will likely be, "How much will that cost?" It's not surprising that people go straight to the money. Understanding the financial impact helps put this seemingly radical and unobtainable idea into relatable terms.

In this chapter, we explain how we arrived at our budget. Although there are lots of online resources and books with more detailed budget breakouts and greater precision, this chapter is intended to help you understand how you may want to approach budgeting in different parts of the world and maximize your money throughout your trip.

When asked, most people guess we spent around $60,000 on the trip and are shocked when we tell them otherwise. We spent $37,000 total for nearly one year of travel. As David says, the trip was about the cost of a midrange sedan and well below what many people spend during a year at home—depending on where you live, of course. The budget you have for your trip will depend on a number of factors: how comfortably you want to live, what matters to you, how quickly or slowly you want to move from place to place, and what parts of the world you plan on visiting. There is no magic number, just as there is no magic route, and your budget is likely to be different from the budgets of other travelers, but we can share the wisdom from our own experiences and those of others to help you stretch your money further and make the most of your time.

MONEY TALKS

Alexandra

Before we left, we dove into research, consulting different sources on average costs for a round-the-world trip. What we found was that a lot of it came down to how comfortably people wanted to travel. A no-frills backpacker could make their way around the world for a year for around $15,000, while many people would spend closer to $45,000 for a similar trip. The differences in budget were based on preferences for lodging, dining, trans-portation, and excursions. We wanted to fall somewhere in the middle. We were accustomed to a certain amount of comfort but also weren't looking for an extended vacation. We were hungry for authenticity and cultural immersion, along with all the local flavors we dreamed of nibbling and sipping as we went. We also wanted to experience a few big-ticket items, like kayaking through Milford Sound in New Zealand, motorcycling the Mae Hong Son loop in northern Thailand, and visiting lots of museums in Paris. Fortunately, David and I were traveling as a couple, which helped us split costs, and were lucky to have friends and family across the globe, which provided us lots of free places to stay.

Taking all of this into account, we settled on our budget of $37,000, which included everything: flights, other transit, accommodations, food, excursions, basic necessities, and gifts for folks back home and people we stayed with along the way. David also had a small budget of $1,000 for personal purchases and special occasions.

I often found myself fixating on the dollars, wanting to dutifully stick to our budget like a Girl Scout intent on earning her merit badges. David helped us maintain perspective, often reminding me that the budget was a noble goal but not something we should let control our lives. He created a few sayings to help me fixate less on the budget, such as, "We won't look back and feel proud of sticking to a number. We will look back and feel proud we had *lived* for a year." We would frequently go way over budget for a couple days or even a week, but those times were countered by stretches where we were well under budget. We decided if we ran out of money earlier than expected, we would simply go home earlier. This helped take the pressure off the budget and keep us present to enjoy our trip.

When David and I decided to take our trip, we didn't have a budget in mind. After aggressively paying off his student loans, David started saving for a shorter but much costlier solo motorcycle adventure. My goal was to match that amount. Although I also had some savings, I was able to make up the difference by selling my Honda Fit, taking on a big freelance job, and greatly reducing my rent by staying with David and his two roommates for a couple months. In my world, everything went very smoothly. We sold my car, my freelance gig was great, rent was cheap, and I got to be with the man I loved so much more.

It was not until we were on our trip that I realized David had been silently freaking out during that time. Things had gone way too fast, riddled with far too much change for him to process what was happening. Months later on a beach in Thailand, David casually brought up how difficult that time was, and I thought to myself, *What is he talking about? That was* blissful! A couple of "How did you not see that?" looks from David were followed by blushing and guilt from me. I guess I had been living in a bit of a romantic fairy tale . . . alone. He tried to comfort me by saying he sincerely felt it had been worth the discomfort. I think we might have laughed about it at some point. I'm not sure I really laughed.

While the logistics of saving for our trip may not have been perfect on both sides, they did enable us to gather enough funds to make the trip work. The budget proved to be an ongoing conversation throughout our journey, and there were definitely moments of tension—mainly when I got too worried about running out of money. It helped that our financials weren't a taboo topic with us, though, probably *because* things had moved so fast at the beginning. Money is often a hot-button topic with couples, but being able to talk openly about our budget enabled me to slowly trust David's financial judgment more and more, and to ultimately trust that everything would work out just fine.

SETTING YOUR BUDGET

The budget can feel like the most daunting part of your trip, but figuring out a rough number is actually a quick exercise. With a few key inputs, you'll be able to get a good sense of how much you can reasonably expect to spend on your trip.

Regional Daily Averages
Your general route is a good starting point to help you wrap your head around how much you can expect to spend in each area. Within your route, each region will have an average daily cost that takes into account your preferred comfort level. We labeled these as "low," "medium," "high," or "superhigh" burn areas.

Below are our averages, which take into account what basic things in each region cost: transportation, accommodation, food and beverages, and miscellaneous, such as basic necessities, excursions and activities, and gifts. These averages are based on a roughly 75/25 split between cities and towns versus countryside, with some regional touring. We wanted to enjoy ourselves and not completely "rough it," so we built a cushion into our daily averages. Rather than trying to stick to these amounts each day, we went for a total average for the entire time we were in a region. In other words, some days were high while others were low. Overall, everything tended to even out.

continued ⟶

REGION	DAILY BUDGET in 2014 (AVERAGE)
India	$35–$75/day (low burn)
Southeast Asia	$35–$90/day (low burn)
Central America	$50–$110/day (medium burn)
Eastern Europe	$65–$100/day (medium burn)
South America	$65–$110/day (medium burn)
Western Europe	$80–$140/day (high burn)
United States	$80–$140/day (high burn)
New Zealand/Australia	$90–$180/day (superhigh burn)
Japan	$110–$200/day (superhigh burn)
United Kingdom	$110–$200/day (superhigh burn)

Your daily averages may look different than these based on the level of comfort you choose, your interests, how much you want to be actively thinking about your budget, and the financial climate of each area when you visit—social and political events can have a big impact on these numbers. It is well worth checking out online resources and frequently updated travel books when establishing your daily averages.

We were more budget-conscious in Europe where luxuries are expensive, but in Southeast Asia and India we gave ourselves much more breathing room. For example, we could make it in Thailand on $20 a day, but by budgeting $70 a day we gave ourselves the freedom to not think about our budget and spend as we wished.

Splitting Your Time

Once you have a sense of your daily averages, you can start to wrap your head around how much time you can afford to spend in each region. We never spent more than two weeks in a "superhigh burn" country and maximized our time in "low" and "medium" burn regions. Based on these daily averages, we ended up spending four and a half months in Southeast Asia and India, a month in Eastern Europe, and three months in Western Europe, interspersing shorter stints in the more expensive places in between. Below is a summary of our rough budget. We included an estimate on "Free Housing & Transit" in order to help quantify what you may need if you do not have a network of people to host you. In most cases, our hosts' homes were significantly nicer than accommodations we would have had otherwise, but this estimate reflects what we think we would have spent on a basic Airbnb, guesthouse room, or something similar.

continued ►—►

Region	Daily Budget (for 2)	Weeks	Total	Free Housing & Transit
United States	$50	6.5	$2,275.00	$(2,400.00)
Central America	$100	1.5	$1,050.00	--
New Zealand/ Australia	$120	3.5	$2,940.00	$(1,200.00)
Southeast Asia	$70	12	$5,880.00	--
Japan	$120	2	$1,680.00	--
India	$55	6	$2,310.00	$(300.00)
Eastern Europe	$75	4.5	$2,362.50	$(1,200.00)
United Kingdom	$120	3.5	$2,940.00	$(700.00)
Western Europe	$110	11.5	$8,855.00	$(1,300.00)
Regional Totals		**51**	**$30,292.50**	**$(7,100.00)**

Other Expenses	Total
David's Personal Stash	$1,000.00
Transportation Costs	$13,000.00
Credit Card Points Savings	$(7,000.00)
Housing Savings	$(7,100.00)
GRAND TOTAL	**$37,292.50**

In Case of Emergency

Always have some emergency cash in USD stashed away. We kept $400 in reserve money for "just in case" moments. We divided it up and hid the money in secret pockets in our backpacks and under the insoles of our shoes.

ROUND-THE-WORLD TICKETS–YES OR NO?

When you decide to take a trip around the world, people will often ask whether you are doing a round-the-world (RTW) ticket. It's a logical conclusion to make, particularly given the branding. RTW tickets range in cost from $6,000 to $7,000 per person with roughly ten destinations available per ticket. RTW tickets require you to book your destinations in advance, limit what carriers you can use, and confine you to a single direction of travel. If headed east, for example, you cannot backtrack west. For us and every other traveler we met, restrictions and advance planning were deal breakers. Moreover, these tickets are expensive. We ended up spending just shy of $6,000 each on our twenty plane tickets, including the long international stretches to and from home, a multi-leg journey to Japan involving flying in and out of smaller airports, and all the regional flights we took back and forth across countries. We also didn't book most of our flights far in advance, apart from the longer and guaranteed-to-be-more-expensive stretches when moving from region to region. On average, we booked flights anywhere from two to six weeks in advance and never ended up being burned on prices.

THE TIME VERSUS MONEY RULE

David

The quicker you move from place to place, the more money you will spend. For example, if you want to see a few cities in a country in two weeks, you will need to pay to get from place to place. Unless you want to spend a significant portion of your time on a slow bus or train, you will most likely opt for quicker, more expensive modes of transport. Once at your destination, you may be tired and want to treat yourself to something easy, which is often costlier. And finally, since you only have a few days, you will want to see and experience everything you can, which often comes with a price tag.

It didn't take us long to notice this and develop the "time versus money rule." Although Alexandra seemed like the more budget-conscious member of our party, we both tend to veer toward frugality. Shortly after our trip had begun, we spent what felt like forever debating whether or not we should purchase a $125 plane ticket from Cambodia to Laos instead of taking a $5 bus. In the end, the extra time at our destination was worth the money.

The rule wasn't just about transportation costs and time; it also had to do with the speed of transport and the density of our agenda. If we wanted to hit a bunch of places in a short amount of time, we needed to accept the fact that we would spend more.

When we decided to add Japan to our itinerary at the last minute, we made our plans with the understanding that two weeks there would simply cost more, not only because of the local economy but also because of the limited time we would have to see multiple places.

On the flip side, when we were looking to take it easy and really get to know a place, we generally spent less. Europe is known for being expensive, but when we decided to spend nine days in Lyon, our time was so relaxing and leisurely that we ended up spending relatively little.

This rule helped guide our decisions throughout our trip, and a couple times it even helped us slow down, which always paid off in the end.

83

TRICKS FOR STRETCHING YOUR BUDGET

A budget may be a finite amount of money, but with a few simple tricks, you'll find you can stretch this pool more than many people would expect. By implementing these tricks into our travel routines, we were able to save thousands of dollars and relieve a lot of the anxiety we felt about sticking with our budget.

1/ Sign Up for Credit Cards with Rewards Programs

There are countless credit cards out there, many of which tempt you with amazing sign-up bonuses and points when you spend on travel and eating out. When you're taking a trip around the world, almost all of the expenses you put on a card are travel and dining related, meaning you rack up points quicker. We strategically signed up for three different credit cards over the course of our trip, timing them at three-month intervals to be able to hit all the different rewards bonuses and use those points for future flights and accommodations. We were so appreciative of NerdWallet's site, where we found the best deals. We then called the companies and asked them to ship our cards internationally for free. Between the three credit cards and points we already had, we ended up saving $5,000 on flights and $2,000 on other travel-related expenses.

Note: We each kept one of the cards after the trip and ended up canceling the others within a year of returning to avoid being hit with the annual fees. The impact to our credit scores for doing this was negligible.

2/ Leverage Your Network

Reach out to friends, family, and friends of friends as you travel to see if they are willing to show you around or host you. Staying with people you have a connection to is not only a great way to save money but also often a richer experience than staying by yourself in a foreign place. Even if you cannot stay with people you know, they will often be enthusiastic guides, introduce you to other locals, and show you places you may not have found otherwise. For the most part, we were amazed by how happy people were to host us and show us their hometowns through their eyes. When we look back, some of the richest experiences we had were in some way due to the help of friends, friends of friends, and family along the way.

3/ Ask for Discounts

Throughout our trip, especially in Europe, we stayed in a lot of Airbnbs. Sometimes we stayed with a host, but most of the time we stayed in our own apartments. People assume hostels are the cheapest option in Europe, but as a couple looking for some privacy, we didn't find this to be true. Airbnb became the most affordable and enjoyable option, particularly with the added cost-savings benefit of being able to cook at home. We would also ask our hosts for a discount. This seems like it would be uncomfortable, but people aren't offended when you ask considerately. Before submitting a booking request, we would send an inquiry to the host and share our story. We would ask for a small discount for a longer stay or offer to clean in exchange for waiving the cleaning fee. These small amounts of money added up, and we always left our hosts a small gift from our travels as a thank-you.

continued ----

4/ Live like the Locals Do

Part of what makes vacations so expensive is the short-term luxury mentality: you are rewarding yourself for working so hard. Vacationers eat out for almost every meal, visit lots of sights, and take quick but more expensive transportation. If you're traveling for an extended period of time, you have the opportunity to mimic the locals. Not only will your budget benefit, but you will also have a richer experience as you dive deeper into the culture. This was especially true for us in Europe.

- **Sleep like Locals Do:** Stay in less touristy neighborhoods. You'll not only save money and escape the tourists, but also discover food gems and greater authenticity.

- **Travel like Locals Do:** Regional airlines outside of the U.S. are amazingly affordable. We flew local airlines all the time, and they were often cheaper than trains. Trains can be one of the very best ways to travel, but they generally require more advanced bookings in order to save. Buses are also a common way to travel and can be quite nice. In Southeast Asia and India we had a couple of excellent bus experiences, and even the buses we took in Europe were pleasant.

- **Eat like Locals Do:** If you want a classic hamburger outside of a Western country, you're going to pay Western prices for it. For example, a burger, fries, and an imported beer in Thailand will cost you about $12 to $16, while pad thai and a local beer will be $3 and way more delicious. Also, avoid tourist traps. Everywhere you go will have restaurants catering to tourists, where the food is generally more expensive and less tasty. Ask locals for their favorite spots and sniff out the places with delicious vibes.

- **Live like Locals Do:** When in Europe, stay in places where you can cook at home and take advantage of the local markets and produce. Going to the market and learning how to cook seasonally is both an awesome cultural experience and budget-friendly.

5/ Know When to Afford Your Luxury

When you're on the road for a long time, you may need "a vacation from your vacation." It's important to take time to rest after being on the go. Between Japan and India, we spent two weeks relaxing on the island of Ko Lanta in southern Thailand—a much-needed break before the intensity of India. When you do take a vacation from your vacation, make sure it's in a place where your money can go further so you can relax and not worry.

A NOTE ON TRACKING YOUR BUDGET
Alexandra

How you monitor your budget on the road often reflects how you keep track of your money at home. In our daily lives, we always had a good sense of what money we had, what we had spent, and what we had saved, but neither of us tracked diligently. However, when we left on the trip, I decided to keep track of everything we spent in a notebook. While we both agreed to this plan, I went deeper down the tracking rabbit hole than David. For nine months, I tracked every expense each day, from a cup of coffee and lunch to a fifty-cent tuk-tuk ride. This generally worked out well, but as the trip went on, and our return date approached, the budget tracking began to produce more stress than reassurance.

Two months before the end of the trip, David encouraged me to loosen up our tracking system. He suggested we try not tracking and see where we netted out at the end of a week. If we were way over budget, we would go back to diligent tracking, but if we were spending roughly the same, we would stop worrying about tracking for the rest of our trip. At the end of the week, we found we had stayed on budget without tracking. I was scared to not track for the rest of the trip, but it was a good test in learning to let go and have faith in our ability to take care of ourselves. If we could do it again, I would track for the first couple weeks of getting to a new region as we adjusted and then assume we would self-govern from there.

TRAVEL ISN'T A LONG VACATION

The average cost of a two-week European vacation for two people is about $6,200. If we had spent like that while in Europe, we would have blown our entire eleven-month budget in less than three months. On our budget we lived surprisingly well. We generally ate what we wanted, stayed in comfortable places, and enjoyed a variety of modes of transportation. We didn't do a lot of sightseeing in the traditional sense, but we really got to know the places we visited. There were only a handful of times throughout our trip when we felt restricted financially, but those were few and far between and paled in comparison to the many moments we felt beyond lucky. We came to see that living on a budget doesn't mean constant sacrifice and missed opportunities. Rather, we saw our budget as an opportunity for us to be more intentional with our time and money.

With yearlong travel you may not have the luxury of having lots of money, but you have the luxury of lots of time. You also have the luxury of not needing to unwind from a stressful job in a finite two-week period. You are where you are to experience that place and learn from its people, and this is a completely incredible mindset to be able to enjoy.

CHAPTER 4

Prepping and Packing

PLANNING IT OUT

Alexandra

David and I are planners. David tends to focus on the high-level "big picture," while I immediately rush to tackle all the logistics. Preparing for a trip around the world proved to be no different. Our need to be prepared for any and all situations throughout the course of a year, and the daunting feeling of thinking through the countless situations we might encounter, butted heads with our desire to be light, easy, and free, jumping off airplanes without checking bags and not feeling burdened by huge packs that made us stick out in a crowd, as if we had a neon sign over our heads screaming "Tourists! Rob them!" These competing wishes created some tension, and as our departure date drew nearer, we began to feel overwhelmed.

Preparing for a trip around the world felt like a massive undertaking when compared to planning for a two-week vacation, but in reality, there was a shocking level of similarity. A lot of the anxieties felt the same. We debated what to pack, wondering what we would want to wear, how weather would impact what we brought, and how light we wanted to keep our bags. We asked many of the same questions we would ask ourselves before a vacation. Should we have a friend collect our mail? What would we do about recurring payments? What did we really need to get done before we left, and what did we really need to bring?

The more we thought about things, the more we read. Packing seemed like a more tangible obstacle to tackle, and we quickly went down a rabbit hole of "optimal travel clothing." David began

scouring the internet for deals on brands we'd never heard of, all of which sounded like characters out of a sci-fi comic series. We stopped listening to ourselves and started drowning in blog chatter. As we made note of all the things we thought we were supposed to bring and do, it started to feel like our packs would be enormous and that there was no way we'd get everything taken care of before we left.

It took actually being on the road for us to learn what we really should have packed and what really needed to be done back home before taking off. In this chapter, we share the lessons we learned about what really needs to be buttoned up at home, what you actually need to pack, and, just as important, what you can let go of and leave behind. These tips will hopefully save you some time, headaches, and unnecessary purchases.

BUTTONING UP

In some ways, leaving the country for a year felt simple, but in other ways, it felt like conquering series after series of to-do lists and decisions. The months leading up to our departure were dense, and we got a lot done. But once we had taken care of our visas for India, gotten our shots, found our backpacks and filled them, signed up for a travel insurance policy, and finalized our housing plan, we realized there wasn't actually much else left we *needed* to do. We could just . . . go. No one was stopping us, and there were no looming deadlines or schedules. We headed into the holiday season feeling more settled and more excited about our upcoming departure. With all the research we had done over the last several months, we felt like we had covered all our bases, and when we finally left the country in January, we left with an assumption that our interactions with life back home would be limited apart from correspondence with friends and family.

Yet despite the research we had done and the coverage plans we had made, a few things slipped through the cracks. Looking back, we had focused more on trip-related logistics and left without really thinking about some of the more practical things in life that were not addressed in any of the blogs and books we read, like vehicle registration renewals and potential hiccups with landlords in a housing-frenzied city like San Francisco. We ended up having to engage with life back home in ways we hadn't expected to, and while unforeseen hurdles are bound to come up, we could have easily avoided a few had we known about them in advance.

95

THE CRITICAL COMPONENTS
TO TAKE CARE OF BEFORE LEAVING

At the end of the day, there are really only a few key things to get done before leaving on your trip. With a solid coverage plan for home in place and a strong sense of your route and budget, the rest can be addressed as you go.

1/ Daily Life Logistics
Even though you may be gone, life back home doesn't stop. The mail still comes, and bills will crop up. Make sure you have a plan in place for managing all the logistics of day-to-day life, which may mean involving a crew of friends and family who are willing to help.

- **Housing and Storage:** If you're going to return to your home base, decide if you want to sublet or rent out your place. If you're not planning on returning, you can put everything in storage and make a plan to stay with family or friends when you get back.

- **Mail:** When you go on a vacation, you can put your mail on hold, but when you're gone for a year, you may miss critical things by doing this. Forward your mail to a trusted friend or family member who can open anything that looks important and email you bills, renewal notices, and the like so you don't get caught off guard, miss a payment, or get nailed with a huge fine while you're traveling.

- **Recurring Payments:** For any recurring payments you have, make sure all credit cards are up to date or automatic withdrawals are set up. Ensure you have enough money in linked bank accounts to cover these payments. If you have a vehicle you're leaving behind, make sure you thoroughly research what the policy is for your annual registration renewal. If you need to renew your registration while you're gone, designate someone else to help take care of this while you're away.

2/ Passport Check

Make sure your passport is up to date and won't expire while you're abroad! At this point, you may be thinking, "well, duh . . ." But you would be surprised how many people get so excited about planning their trip and don't look at their passport until a few weeks out, only to find it's expired. Another thing we didn't know before we left was that some countries, like Laos, Myanmar, China, and Indonesia, require your passport to be valid for six months from the date of entry. India requires your passport to be valid for six months from the date you apply for a visa.

continued ←→

3/ Visas

Research the countries that require advance visa applications and make sure you're giving yourself enough time to take care of the paperwork. There are agencies in the U.S. that can help you do some visa applications, and certain countries, like India, now require you go through an agency. You can easily apply for some visas while on the road, so bring along several extra passport-size photos with you.

TIP: ▶ When taking your extra photos for travel visas, try not to smile. Some countries have different photography requirements, and you wouldn't want to be rejected because of grinning from ear to ear.

4/ A Solid Backpack

As far as geeky gear goes, this is the only area to pay attention to. Invest in a REALLY GOOD backpack. Trust us on this one. Make sure the pack is very comfortable, is the right size, and feels great on your back. We were not "backpacking," but there are many times when you will need to walk for a while before arriving at your destination and will be appreciative of a contained, secure, and comfortable backpack.

TIP 1: ▶ Make sure your backpack will fit in the average overhead compartment on an airplane. Checking luggage around the world will be a waste of time and money, and opens you up to potential theft, so you want to ensure your pack can easily come on the plane with you. Our backpacks were 35 liters standard and could be expanded to 40 liters if needed. We found they fit in every single overhead bin we encountered.

TIP 2: ▶ If you can, find a backpack with a built-in rain fly. Even if you aren't planning on being in places with lots of rainy weather, the rain fly is incredibly useful. It served as great protection the few times we decided to check our packs, as it kept all of our straps contained and the bags clean. It also became an extra layer of security during transit. In train stations, for example, risks of theft are much higher, but if you cover your backpack with the rain fly, you automatically create one more deterrent for potential thieves.

TIP 3: ▶ Find a backpack with multiple entry points. Our backpacks not only opened from the top but also unzipped in the front, which was very convenient when packing and unpacking.

TIP 4: ▶ Consider a backpack with less widely known branding. We went with Gregory, a solid but less commercial brand in the States, and what we liked about these packs was not only their incredible form and functionality but also their complete lack of obvious branding. We felt less likely to be targets for theft, and the nondescript, neutral colors helped us blend in more.

continued ⤙

5/ Vaccinations and Meds

Make an appointment at a local travel clinic and get all the shots you'll need based on your general route and the regions you'll be visiting. If you have insurance with your employer, do this while you are under their coverage. You may also want to stock up on some emergency meds, like Cipro and malaria pills if you decide to take them.

6/ Travel Insurance

Getting travel insurance is a must. First of all, it's really affordable. Second, it will cover any medical emergencies that may arise, including an airlift evacuation if needed. Finally, if something gets lost or stolen while you're on the road, your travel insurance will cover the cost of replacement. There are several providers out there, but we had a great experience with World Nomads.

7/ International Driver's License

We always wondered if an international driver's license was actually necessary, but when a friend in England offered to lend us his car and his insurance company required one of us to have an international driver's license, we realized there are in fact some situations when it's needed. While you may not think you'll be driving at all, you never know, and it's both easy and inexpensive to get an international driver's license. AAA can take care of it for you quite quickly. It's much easier to get your international driver's license before you leave, but it's still possible to get one while on the road. You can mail in your application to AAA along with two recent passport photos (signed on the back), the fee in check form ($20 as of 2018), and a photocopy of both sides of your U.S. driver's license, but if you go with this option, make sure to leave a big window of time for getting the international license back. You'll also need to have an address for AAA to mail the license to in a few weeks' time. Alternatively, you can have someone in the States go to AAA on your behalf with all the necessary materials and send the international driver's license to you, which could be somewhat faster depending on how they mail it to you.

We Look Ridiculous

Sydney, Australia

ALEXANDRA

33.8688° S, 151.2093° E

David and I had been on the road for three weeks when we realized what a mistake it had been to bring adventure pants. Every website and guidebook had strongly encouraged all sorts of quick-drying, lightweight clothing, and we had succumbed to the pressure, packing what could only be described as a cross between yoga pants and a parachute. We committed to the adventure pants, wearing them day in and day out for the two weeks we spent traveling around New Zealand, but when we got to Sydney, Australia, *we knew we just weren't adventure pants people, even the round-the-world-travelers versions of ourselves.* Sure, our pants dried surprisingly fast, and they weighed practically nothing, but they made us feel unattractive and like obvious tourists. They also swished when we walked, which didn't add to any allure they might have held before we left.

We hit a low point when we were spending the day in the hip, stylish, and incredibly attractive Sydney neighborhood of Bondi Beach. We had been introduced to some locals through a friend back home, and these newfound acquaintances had invited us to a lawn bowling birthday party. After a stroll along the unbelievably gorgeous coastline, we arrived at one of the most picturesque sights one could imagine for a party. The bowling lawn was a vibrant green outcrop overlooking the sea below. David and I quickly identified the gathering of very well-dressed good-looking people as the party we were attending, and as we looked down at our slightly shimmery adventure pants and quick-drying shirts, we had never felt frumpier. For a moment, we considered turning around and not going. We ended up having a really nice time at the party despite some gracious but sideways looks at our ridiculous attire that whispered of a week on safari, but it was a turning point for us. We did not want to spend the next ten months looking and feeling like idiots. When we arrived in Singapore the next day, we found the nearest H&M and purchased cheap, lightweight jeans and regular shirts. We instantly felt more like ourselves.

UNPACKING WHAT TO PACK

There is no singular packing list, as preferences and routes vary, but after living out of our backpacks for a year, we have a few opinions on what ended up feeling necessary, what was nice to have, and what proved to be nothing more than extra weight. Your route will serve as the foundation for what you pack, but here are a few tips to help filter and focus.

TIP 1: ▷ Make sure all your basic bases are covered: you'll want flexibility for hot weather and cold weather, and rainy weather and dry weather, while knowing that depending on your route, you are not likely to encounter many extremes throughout most of your journey.

TIP 2: ▷ Dress how you would dress at home. Pack what's natural and comfortable for you. If you're a T-shirt and jeans type of person at home, you'll likely be a T-shirt and jeans person while on the road. The one thing to keep in mind is weight. You may need to explore lighter versions of what you typically wear to keep your load more manageable.

TIP 3: ▷ Most clothes are disposable. You can swap things out as you go to add some variety and help you feel more blended in with the local scene. The clothing in your backpack when you return will likely not be the same as what you packed when you left.

TIP 4: ▶ Bring a few favorite pieces of clothing and accessories that remind you of home. These could be a beloved T-shirt, a hat, a scarf, or a pair of earrings that make you feel really special. Having these small pieces of home can be comforting and provide a sense of familiarity in a world of unknowns.

TIP 5: ▶ In many countries, it's harder to find shoes in larger sizes. If your feet are larger than size 11/12, you may want to come more prepared.

DOING LAUNDRY ON THE ROAD

Take a quiet moment now to appreciate how incredible dryers are; they are responsible for supersoft towels on your face in the morning, comforting undershirts throughout the day, and heavenly sheets at night. Based on our experience, air-drying is the norm outside of the U.S. This means crispy laundry that never smells quite as clean.

We assumed we would be washing a lot of clothes ourselves. Generally, a washing machine was easily accessible, but several times we hand-washed our clothes in sinks or showers. For this reason, we recommend always carrying a small amount of soap and a clothesline.

At points throughout our trip, we did outsource our laundry. Through Southeast and Central Asia and India, it's easy to find people who will do your laundry for you at a very cheap price, but in our experiences, our clothes often came back still damp and not smelling particularly clean. We found ourselves rewashing quite often until we got to Europe. Once in Europe, most everywhere we stayed had washing machines and drying racks, so doing laundry regularly was easy.

THE PACKING LIST

As you pack, keep in mind two things:

1. Is it worth the weight? This is a good question to ask yourself for every item you consider. It also reinforces what your priorities are. In retrospect, we regret not bringing a portable speaker with us, as music is a big part of our lives and listening directly off our phone was less than mood setting.

2. If you go with a smaller backpack, roughly 35 to 40 liters, try to only fill it to 60 to 70 percent of capacity. This way, you'll easily be able to carry on your backpack on all flights and have space for things you pick up as you go.

THE PACKING LIST

Quick-drying underwear
(6–7 pairs per person)

Down jacket (packable)

Windbreaker (packable)

Lightweight rain jacket (packable)

Moisture-wicking socks
(5 pairs)

Practical walking shoes
(1 pair)

Lightweight thermals
(top and bottom)

Nicer shoes (1 pair)

Flip-flops or sandals
(1 pair)

T-shirts (2–3)

Tank tops (2)

Short-sleeved button-down
or blouse (1)

Long-sleeved button-down
or blouse (1)

Shorts (1 pair)

Pants (1 pair)

Long-sleeved warm top (1)–
a lightweight sweatshirt or sweater

Dresses (1–2)

Bathing suit (1)

Scarf

Warm hat

Quick-dry towel (1)–
extra-large size

Bandana

Sunglasses

Portable clothesline

First-aid kit

DIY pharmacy of useful things that are harder to get around the world (ibuprofen, Sudafed, Cipro, malaria pills, Benadryl, charcoal pills, Imodium, probiotics, chamomile tea, Neosporin)

Nail clippers

Menstrual cup (tampons are often hard to come by around the world)

Lightweight water bottle

Zip-top freezer bags (2 quart sized, 2 gallon sized)

Water sterilizing "pen"

Money belt—for travel days

Spork

Foldable shoulder bag

Compression sack— for minimizing clothing volume in your pack

Lightweight metal cup (which also doubles as good storage space)

Note: A lot of folks recommend a small daypack, which we initially brought, but rarely used as they were not comfortable for long distances and stood out in small towns and cities. When needed, we found you can easily and cheaply purchase these, but the shoulder bag proved to be an essential.

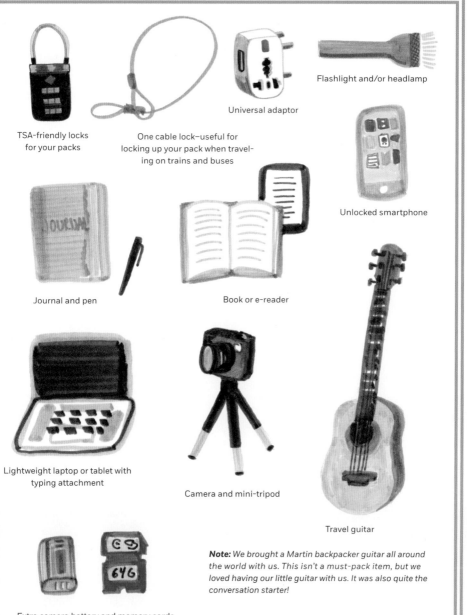

TSA-friendly locks
for your packs

One cable lock—useful for
locking up your pack when traveling on trains and buses

Universal adaptor

Flashlight and/or headlamp

Unlocked smartphone

Journal and pen

Book or e-reader

Lightweight laptop or tablet with
typing attachment

Camera and mini-tripod

Travel guitar

Extra camera battery and memory cards

Note: *We brought a Martin backpacker guitar all around
the world with us. This isn't a must-pack item, but we
loved having our little guitar with us. It was also quite the
conversation starter!*

WHEN NOT TO SKIMP

While a lot of what you bring in your pack doesn't have to be high priced or high-end, there were a few items we felt were worth more of an investment. These were the things that proved invaluable to us when we were on the road, the items we continuously felt grateful for having.

- **ExOfficio® underwear:** Of all the techy clothing we read about, ExOfficio® underwear proved to be the garment that truly made a difference. They are lightweight, easy to wash, dry overnight, and pack up really small. They are also incredibly comfortable.

- **Lightweight thermals:** Thermals take up little space in your pack but make all the difference in a variety of climates. When it's cold, they give you an extra layer of warmth without the bulk, and when it's hot but buggy, they make for a more breathable sleeping attire option.

- **Down jacket:** Our down jackets proved to be invaluable. When packed into their own pockets, they were great makeshift pillows, and when the weather got nippy, they provided instant but lightweight warmth.

- **Windbreaker:** A lightweight windbreaker that packs into its own pocket is another invaluable item. You can carry it with you at all times, and it can provide an effective temperature shield if the weather suddenly turns.

- **Lightweight rain jacket:** While you may not encounter a lot of rain, you'll want to be comfortable and dry when you do. Umbrellas are awkward to carry, whereas a packable rain jacket fits neatly into your backpack.

- **Moisture-wicking socks:** You're going to want your feet to be in the best condition they can be in during your trip, which is a challenge when you're constantly on them. Having proper footwear is one step, but having high-quality socks is another. Moisture-wicking socks are durable, quick-drying, and breathable. You don't even have to wash them after every use.

- **Practical walking shoes:** You'll want a pair of shoes that feel great to walk and stand in but that you also like and feel are versatile enough to take you wherever you want to go.

- **Ziploc® freezer bags:** These came in handy for so many things, from storing medical supplies to keeping dirty laundry separate. Make sure to get the name-brand kind because those *last*. Several years later, the Ziploc® bags we used on our trip are still functioning.

PACKED AND READY

As we spent more time on the road, we became packing ninjas. We began to understand how little we actually needed to live and dress comfortably. We developed systems for optimizing the organization of our packs. We got to a point where the essentials were at the ready, and we could pack our completely unpacked backpacks in just under fifteen minutes. We kept our loads light, and when we cinched down our packs as much as possible, we never struggled with fitting them into an overhead compartment. During our travels, we would see twenty-year-olds weighed down with seventy-liter packs towering over their heads and overstuffed daypacks worn on their chests, or nervously waiting for a checked bag to emerge from the mouth of a luggage belt. We would marvel at the bulk they carried and wonder what could possibly be in there.

While there were times when we got sick of a particular shirt or felt constantly underdressed in cities like Milan and Paris, we were glad to have light loads. We were comforted by how contained our packs were, that everything we carried fit neatly on our backs. Life felt simpler.

SECTION II

ON THE ROAD

CHAPTER 5

Adjusting to Life on the Road

Leaving home is a special moment. You know you are on the brink of something, at the beginning of an adventure. Everything beyond that point is generally an unknown, even if you have a plan. Yet one thing is certain: your individual experience will be unlike anybody else's.

Every traveler will have his or her unique transition to life on the road. Some people we met had easily left everything behind and transitioned into traveling effortlessly. Whatever challenges they might have had before their departure didn't seem to follow them. Other people had left to actively process what they were grappling with at home or to work through something major. A few people had left with the desire to not return to any semblance of the life they had led before and instead pursue a course entirely different.

Because everyone is different and traveling for countless unique reasons, it would be impossible to offer advice on adjusting to the journey. Each adjustment experience is going to be singular. We can, however, share what was most meaningful to us: stories. In this chapter, we share a few stories about how we adjusted to life on the road and a look into what we learned along the way.

121

On the Edge

Sámara, Costa Rica

DAVID

9.8820° N, 85.5290° W

Alexandra was talking to me, but I was unable to listen. I couldn't seem to register her words or much of anything else around me. Anxiety was swirling in the lower spaces of my stomach, but the rest of my body felt lifeless. My thoughts were boring. I had no insight on the conversation or anything relevant to the moment. An hour ago I had been searching Google for articles on early onset Alzheimer's disease. For weeks I had felt as though someone let the line out on the anchor of my mind. "Sorry love," I told Alexandra. "I can't hear anything right now. I'm not feeling myself." I could tell she was mildly offended and sensed she felt responsible for whatever it was I was going through. I had a visceral response to make her feel better. I said something ineffectual like a drunk apologizing to whatever was around him after bumping into a wall or a piece of furniture: "Sorry. Just ignore me."

I drank a third cup of coffee, and my long stares into nothing were disrupted by caffeine jitters. "Let's get dressed and go to the beach," I said as I began to stand up. As we walked back to our room, I was distracted by the incredible amount of wildlife around us. Several types of birds, lizards large and small, unusual insects, and monkey-like mammals moved around us, and the hotel cat appeared to be ushering us to our door. I callously registered the beauty of the moment as though I'd need to report back on the details later.

After getting dressed, we walked hand in hand down a path leading to the ocean and came upon a few concrete buildings. They could either have been part of a home or a makeshift restaurant. I felt nervous we would need to speak to strangers, as the path led through the property. I wasn't in the mood for conversation, but the alternative of forging our way through the jungle appeared even less comforting. Deciding on the path, my energy shifted, and my internal monologue grew hyperactive. *Why do I not feel like I am on vacation? This looks a lot like vacation. A really nice one too . . . What about this situation is not awesome and totally relaxing?*, I thought to myself as we quickly approached what proved to be a restaurant.

A lovely young couple, presumably the owners, greeted us, and I lost track of my train of thought. I quickly transitioned to asking them all sorts of questions. Our conversation was fluid and jovial as I asked about where they came from and what they were up to in Costa Rica. I sensed Alexandra was a bit uneasy, and I assumed it was because her practically mute space cake of a boyfriend just became Mr. Social at the drop of a hat. "Would you like a drink?" they asked, and we accepted.

We sat on a wooden picnic bench overlooking the ocean. I fixed my gaze on the label of my beer that was slowly coming off from the condensation. My mind returned to some of the themes that had come up on our way here and then landed on something that felt undeniable: *not knowing is not a problem, it is your solution.* Agitated as well as liberated by the thought, I distracted myself. Looking back behind me, I saw the jungle's edge and noticed the work this young couple had done to keep it from enveloping their little establishment. Alexandra had wandered off toward the ocean, and I watched her as she explored the shore, stopping to sit on a rock near a fire pit and looking out over the waves.

I looked over to my left and made eye contact with a large brown dog. Although he was without a collar, he didn't seem threatening. He came toward me, and I could see he had kind, dark eyes. He performed a couple of false starts toward the ocean; it was clear he wanted me to play with him. I am allergic to dogs, so I generally do not accept these sorts of invites, but given my state of mind at the time, I felt compelled. The dog led me in Alexandra's general direction, and she got up from her rock and joined us. She inquired about the dog's origins, to which I shrugged and replied, "He seems sweet." I grabbed a stick and threw it down the beach. It got caught up in a couple waves crashing in, but the dog quickly snatched it up. Without any impulse to return it, he carried the stick high and looked almost triumphant while leading us down the beach. After some time, he cut up to a shady spot under a tree that seemed quite familiar to him. *With our new friend by our side, we relaxed and for the first time let all that was around us sink in.* I could tell we both sensed a wildness within the dense jungle behind us, but we focused on the contrasting calm energy of the blue ocean ahead. I felt a sense of rebellion toward the moment and an impulse to undermine its simplicity with chatter, but I held back. By the time the breeze dried our sweat, our dog leader roused us, and we followed him back to the restaurant. I expected the dog to have a plan for some food as payment for his tour, but when we got closer, he took off, running down the beach and into the jungle without a goodbye.

Back at the restaurant, Alexandra and I each sat on a bench and quietly watched the colors of the sky slowly begin to morph. The light angled and brought out shadows as well as a chill in the air. We looked at each other like we both had good news to share. I reached out and took her hand.

We sat together silently, and I returned to my thoughts. I realized that I feared being unclear about what I was doing on this journey, so I attempted to ground myself. *I was here to fulfill a lifelong desire to explore the world, meet people, and learn new and amazing things.* I was also here to question my career choices and give myself the chance to make better ones going forward. I was here to be more real and more honest than I had been with myself or anyone else. I was here to do all this with a woman I hardly knew but had loved from the start, in a relationship that could last another week or my lifetime. *I know what I am doing,* I thought to myself, but before the words settled in, I realized they were what I had needed in order to leave. What I needed now was to wake up and arrive in my new way of living. I needed to let go of what I knew and embrace what I did not.

Meeting Yourself

New Zealand

ALEXANDRA

36.8485° S, 174.7633° E

I have always struggled with letting go of mistakes I've made or regrets from the past. It is a side effect of my long struggle with anxiety. A mix of genes, my upbringing, and traumatic life events resulted in my having some high-strung instincts to control and worry. When we boarded our first one-way flight to New Zealand, I felt a glimmer of hope that perhaps this time, I could finally leave that tightly wound person behind. That by taking this dramatic step I would free myself from the manifestations of these instincts: self-reproach, a compulsion to perform, and excessive planning. *It took me roughly a week to recognize that the traveling version of myself was not miraculously much different, and it took another four months before I found a way to be comfortable with that realization.*

The first week after leaving the States was relatively smooth because an underlying feeling of shock infused everything. On our first morning in New Zealand, I lay in bed looking up at an unfamiliar ceiling and felt the gravity of literally being on the other side of the world. I had never been this far away from home. Traveling across the United States and Costa Rica felt like a lightweight entry into traveling while this felt *real*. During the five days we spent on the North Island of New Zealand, we bound ourselves to each other and moved about in a semi-dream state. I felt in awe of what we were doing. An incredibly generous family friend had offered us not only her beach house up north but also her car and several days' worth of groceries. Feeling so taken care of gave us a sense of comfort as we embarked on our first small adventure. That time was easy. We drove through gorgeous landscapes, cooked simple and delicious meals, discovered beaches where we were more often than not alone, and held each other close at night. I felt free and suspended in mid-air but was also afraid of what would happen when my feet touched the ground.

It wasn't until we met up with two friends taking a shockingly similar trip to ours but in reverse order that I took my first stumble. We were taking a ten-day road trip through the South Island together, and everyone was excited to experience even a fraction of the beauty we had heard so much about: water that glowed turquoise even when the sky was overcast, mountains that whispered of fairy tales, and fiords that made you feel smaller than an ant. We wanted to experience it all. Perhaps it was our highly structured itinerary or the hefty New Zealand price tags contrasting with our meager budget, but I began to feel the familiar tug of anxiety. The course we had mapped out for our road trip also felt similar to the one we had taken in the States. Our days were spent mostly driving, and our collective exhaustion quickly mounted. Distances that had appeared small and doable on the map were taking twice as long to cover in reality. Even though everyone else wanted to slow down, I felt an irrational sense of obligation to the plan. I could feel myself becoming more and more irritating as I reminded David about how long we still had until our next destination on the road trip, but the more he pulled away, the more anxious I became. I fell into a vicious cycle I was ill-equipped to break. Fixating on our itinerary became the outlet for all my nervous energy. It felt less painful than ruminating on how my uptight energy was ruining the trip or wondering about whether David's feelings for me were changing.

As we made our way through the South Island, I could feel a distance growing between David and me. At first I thought the gap was because of our grueling pace or introducing two new people to our crew so soon into our trip, but as we continued south, I couldn't help but think the distance I felt was about something else. The further he pulled away, the more desperately I tried to hold on to him. I was panicked. As crazy as it may sound, our new love had felt unquestionable to me; I had taken this leap of faith into the unknown in part because of it. David began to vacillate between reserved coldness and tender connection. The logical part of me was able to take a step back and recognize a new relationship under so much pressure would likely experience a couple speed bumps, but my emotions felt otherwise. I began to question if David still loved me. When he looked at me sometimes, I could feel him questioning me, questioning what I was saying, how I was acting, or what I was doing.

I felt desperate and clingy and needy, but the more I tried to calm myself down, the worse it became. My subconscious took over as I began to perform in ways I thought David would prefer or would make me the partner he needed. Unlike many other people in my life before him, David was more repelled by this performance than by how I had been acting before.

After about a week, we settled in for a few nights at a quaint waterfront camping village at Lake Wanaka near the epic Milford Sound. With evening descending, I walked to the end of the pier in search of some clarity. As the sun disappeared behind the mountains framing the lake, I watched the sky darken and illuminate with a magnificent peppering of stars. I looked up into the never-ending expansiveness of the sky and felt the sickening grip of fear on my heart. Tears stung at the back of my eyes, and I felt caught between complete awe of the surrounding beauty and hopelessness in the pit of my stomach. It had been hard enough to embark on this adventure with all the skepticism I'd felt from family and friends back home, and now this layer of doubt from David took me over the top. I was caught in the story that actions I had taken back home were "catching up to me," that my messy puddle-jumping past was haunting me and making David question who I really was. I felt disappointed in myself for not becoming the carefree person I had hoped to become. I couldn't believe we were only a few weeks into the "no return" part of the adventure, and I had already begun to fumble.

Night had fallen, and warm yellow lights began to spring up in homes on the other side of the lake. They looked kind and comforting. The stars were endless and dense, leaving little room for blackness. I closed my eyes and breathed in the cool, refreshing air. When I opened my eyes, a brighter light streaked across the sky—a shooting star. Reaching for the comforts and nostalgia of childhood, I held my breath and made a wish, feeling a quiet sense of hope wash over me. There was a real chance everything could end that night: the trip, our fledgling relationship, and my belief in myself to overcome the things holding me down. Even knowing this, I had faith we would continue and that I could overcome my fears. I sat on the end of the pier for a while longer until the outlines of the mountains melted into the dark sky. When I heard footsteps behind me, I knew without looking that it was David. He sat next to me, our legs dangling over the end of the pier, and we sat together quietly, watching the lights flicker in the houses across the lake. We talked a bit, and it was clear my concerns were accurate and shared. Somewhere between something I knew and something he said, *I recognized that the only way I could move forward and be present on this trip would be to let go and accept myself.*

The next morning we woke up early and drove to Milford Sound. One of our splurges had been a kayaking tour of the sound. Upon arrival we were pleasantly surprised with a free upgrade to a longer, more in-depth tour. It felt like a gift, and we took it as one. We were

taken twenty-one kilometers out in a speedboat to where the sea met the sound. With the engine quiet, we could hear nothing but the gentle lapping of the waves. We were paired up in kayaks and began our journey back with two guides leading the way. I had never felt so small. The cliffs on either side towered over us while the deep, black water beneath seemed to go on forever. About halfway back, we arrived at a magnificent waterfall. It was staggering in its tallness and ferocity. The guides told us it was twice the height of Niagara Falls, which was astonishing given it originated from a point only a third of the way up the cliff. The guides also explained that if you paddled hard enough, you could fight the powerful wind and current coming off the falls and get quite close to the bottom. Although the force would be too great to actually get right under the falls, a quick turn at the last moment of forward momentum would send you catapulting back into calm waters. They then gave everyone a chance to give it a go. For reasons unknown, David and I really gave this challenge our all. Although I could hear the guides warning us that a false move would send us flying into the rocks, I was surprisingly not scared. We began to paddle, and as we felt the stunning intensity of the wind and current push us back, we fell into connected strokes, working together as a team. David yelled instructions over the roar of the waterfall, and I paddled harder than I thought possible. Although this was by far my most "extreme sports" moment, my mind felt clear and calm listening to David's voice and trusting his prompts. The waterfall was immense, the sound of crashing water was deafening, and the winds felt like a hurricane. We were soaked as we neared the thunderous base, and as we made what felt like perfectly synchronized strokes, we aligned ourselves to turn just shy of the tumult of the cascade. We were shot out like a cannonball, eyes wide open and smiling broadly. It was euphoric.

To our surprise, our guides greeted us with faces of shock and awe. "You guys are crazy!" they laughed, saying they had never expected us to get quite so close. David seemed surprised by their response, as I think he thought he was just following instructions. I felt exhilarated and connected again to David. When I turned around to smile at him, I didn't feel afraid.

As the weeks went on, things began to get easier. Leaving the more familiar world of New Zealand and Australia for the chaos, heat, and newness of Southeast Asia felt oddly comforting. Because everything around me was so utterly different and unknown, I felt instantly more alive and present. The instinct to get lost in my thoughts was usurped by the bigger pull to see and experience everything around me. I didn't feel afraid hanging on to the sides of tuk-tuks as we whizzed through dense streets without any semblance of traffic laws. Although David still reminded me quite often that it was okay, I felt more comfortable not making so many plans, booking a room for one or two nights before deciding whether to stay in a place for a while or move on to the next. As our pace began to naturally slow, I could feel myself slowing down too, and a couple months in, when the charming allure of Luang Prabang, Laos, sucked us in for a two-week stay, I began to really feel like a traveler.

Letting go of the expectations I held for myself would continue to be as much of a journey throughout the trip as the trip itself. Two sayings often came to me: "No matter where you are, there you are" as well as "If you travel far enough, you'll meet yourself." I began to see that the trip wasn't about discovering a new version of myself; rather, it was about being more accepting of who I already was.

BALANCING PLANNING AND
RESEARCH ON THE ROAD

While a long trip is inherently flexible, the right amount of planning can bring great rewards. Too much planning can waste time and cause unnecessary restriction, but too little planning often results in needless runaround and wasted money. When done right, planning is a tool to help you save time, hassle, and money, as well as get the most out of your experience.

We also found that the right amount of research not only gave us a leg up on where we wanted to stay and areas we wanted to explore, but also enhanced our general experience of a place. Knowing a little about the culture, history, and language of a country or city before arriving enabled quicker engagement and contextualization.

Through our experiences, we developed a few simple tricks to help navigate when and how to plan while on the road.

1/ Do Your Research on the Go:
During the stretches of time spent in transit from one place to another, we settled into a routine where we would read the Wikipedia pages on the country as well as cities we planned on visiting. We were often shocked at the quality of each entry and were always sure to read at least the history and culture sections. They provided us with a free, readily available crash course on the basics of a place and its people. Using transit periods for research not only made the most of our time but also helped us get excited for what was to come.

2/ Planning Days:

After several frustrating and exhausting evenings spent planning on our computer, we decided to formalize the process. Rather than peppering out our planning across a couple days, we would dedicate an afternoon or morning to one planning session. By the time we were ready to plan our next destination, we were usually familiar with wherever we happened to be and had the time to find a café or bar with not only an internet connection but also great atmosphere. We also gave ourselves a time limit, which helped us be decisive and focused. This technique proved invaluable for helping us stay present and not get too caught up in our next stop before leaving the current one.

Driving the Loop

Chiang Mai, Thailand

DAVID

18.7061° N, 98.9817° E

It was almost seven in the morning, and Alexandra was sleeping peacefully next to me. The sun was creating sharp, bright lines across the room as it angled through the old wooden shutters. The air was warm and smelled like dry wood, tuk-tuk exhaust, and fresh cut fruits. Our little corner was beginning to bustle, and the energy felt kinetic. Chiang Mai was waking up. I heard Tony chatting downstairs as he took orders and Mae rattling pans as she prepared breakfast. I didn't want to wake Alexandra, but given that she sleeps like a retired spy, I knew my efforts at not waking her were likely to be futile. Trying my best to be silent, I slowly walked across the room and opened the rickety old door leading to a narrow balcony.

"Where are you going?" Alexandra sprang forward before her eyes were even all the way open.

"Just to the balcony," I replied as I looked back to see her relaxing her muscles and getting comfy again.

"We have a big day today. Are you excited?" she asked, to which I replied, "I really am."

After some time watching the traffic pass and attempting to follow the tangle of wiring linking the buildings around me, I wandered downstairs. We had been staying in this old traditional Thai building for about a week, but it already felt like home. Tony greeted me, giving me a look that explained what he was about to say, and I replied before he found his words. "Yeah . . . granola would be awesome, thank you." I sat down and waved to Mae, who was cooking just a few feet from my seat. Several minutes later, Alexandra joined me and noted how unusual it was to have me downstairs first. I felt an unfamiliar mix of excitement and peace and wanted to tell her about it, but saying that would have made this simple feeling contradictory and complex. Instead, I simply said, "I cannot wait to get on the bike."

Tony's Big Bikes had been recommended by a good friend in San Francisco, as was the Mae Hong Son route we were about to embark on. From what I had learned, it was an endlessly windy and picturesque route through some of the most beautiful country in northern Thailand. I had been missing motorcycle riding immensely.

After breakfast we strolled down the street to Mountain Coffee, the beloved coffee stand we had found on our second morning here. "What would you like today? Two cappuccinos?" asked our thoroughly eccentric and loveably rude coffee roaster and barista. He was giving me a cockeyed mischievous look, which immediately made me smile. I replied with an enthusiastic, "Yes, please!" to which he exclaimed, "Oh, good, I love taking your money!"

His family grew the beans in the mountains about an hour's drive north, and he roasted them here in the city using wood fire and a self-modified cement mixer. Beneath his multipatterned garb and

Technicolor hat was a brilliant and curious man. A few days earlier he had invited us to roast coffee with him, an invitation we had happily accepted. Like himself, his operation felt completely self-made and totally unique. Alexandra and I had been quite taken by his eccentric and lovable personality and were impressed with the life he had carved out for himself.

Chatting a bit about our upcoming adventure, he continued in his morning patter and asked, "So I won't be able to take your money over the next few days then?" He slid our coffees across the counter to us. I shook my head, then looked down to notice he had drawn a lady with large bare breasts in the foam of my coffee and a cowboy in Alexandra's. "Safe travels. Come back so I can take more of your money," he said with a look that revealed his genuinely soft and caring nature. We drank our coffees quickly and as we waved goodbye, Alexandra said, "Don't miss us too much! We won't be gone long."

We strolled back down the lane to our guesthouse, where we packed up our bags and tidied up the room. I got great satisfaction from our ability to pack and unpack quickly. Beyond the gratification of being organized and tidy, our minimal packs felt symbolic of how we valued our time. *Our time belonged to us, belonged to living and experiencing what life had to offer us that day; it didn't belong to my stuff. Within thirty minutes of leaving the coffee shop, Alexandra and I were in a tuk-tuk on our way to a new adventure.*

I had begun mentally riding motorcycles around the age of three. Utilizing my index and middle fingers as wheels, my stable of motorcycles was always with me. Up and down the banisters, over kitchen counters, and even some off-roading on the wide-wale corduroy of our couch—I could ride anywhere. Inside my little-boy imagination, the bike was realer than real, and to me, my tiny voice sounded like the roar of a finely tuned engine. Heeding the pleas of all who loved me, I ignored the voice inside until I couldn't. Twenty-two years later, I quit a job I hated and spent every penny of my savings on a stunning red 1974 BMW R90/6. This move symbolized the start of my pursuing the things I loved, even if this choice and further ones were seen as less than smart by people in my life.

About four hours later, Alexandra and I were fulfilling a near-lifelong dream of mine. We were exploring the glorious unknown on a perfectly running and maintained motorcycle, ripping around roads that were smooth and never straight. The only difference between dream and reality was I was not alone on this adventure. I had Alexandra there with me, fearlessly leaning deeper and deeper into the turns as we adjusted to riding together and our surroundings. It had not been part of my plan, but as was the case with nearly every truly incredible thing, it never could have been. I had hoped to feel this way someday in my life but hadn't expected it. The feeling was far from needed, but I would have given all I had to keep it if it was threatened. In that moment, I could without a doubt say all the bullshit life brings was worth it, that I had no regrets and a partner in the realest sense of the word. It was a glorious mix of presence, life, and love.

Krishna, Krishna

Vrindavan, India

ALEXANDRA

27.5650° N, 77.6593° E

"Leave your shoes here," the driver said, pointing at the floor of the auto-rickshaw. Our friends removed their shoes without hesitation, but as I looked around, taking in the chaos of the street, the meandering cows, flower peddlers selling garlands of marigolds, a street vendor frying *pakoras*, I wavered. I looked at David, who seemed to be feeling similarly, but with our friends waiting, we took off our shoes and placed them inside the auto-rickshaw, wondering if they would be there when we returned.

We set off down the nearest alley, a narrow street made all the narrower by the throngs of people and animals choking the passageway. It was the end of our first full day in India, and we were walking barefoot down the streets. My mind was reeling. There was so much happening around me I could barely focus on one element before darting to the next. Marigold-robed sadhus, Hindi holy men, lined the alley, bowls extended with begging hands. Laughing children ran past. Monkeys stalked us overhead, climbing nimbly on a tangle of electrical lines and pissing into the twilight. The air was thick with the smells of urine, spices, incense, and sweat. The alley hummed, and as I followed closely behind David and his friends, gingerly placing one foot in front of the other in a desperate attempt to avoid stepping on shit of unknown origin, I could feel my mind trying to work its way around what was happening but finding itself unable to do so.

When we landed in Delhi the evening before, David and I had been buzzing with a hesitant excitement. We had both always dreamed of going to India, and thanks to my undying devotion to the Beatles and our mutual love for the film *The Darjeeling Limited*, we had cultivated a deeply ingrained sense of romance around the country— one that wouldn't seem to abandon us, no matter how many India horror stories we had heard in our months on the road leading up to our time there. I was also carrying the chip of not wanting to seem like yet another female pilgrim to the temple of her personal India transformation story. I'd had a visceral reaction to the cause-oriented, white-privileged, female narcissists who seemed drawn to India, and I was terrified of coming across as one to every person I shared my excitement over India with.

I wanted to love India, though, and my intention to do so was stronger than ever once we had arrived. We were staying with Saahil, David's friend from business school, and his family for a few days in Delhi before setting off on our own, and Saahil welcomed us to India with a humbling level of hospitality and generosity. He sent one of his family's drivers to the airport to pick us up, gave us a prepaid

Indian SIM card, and had booked train tickets. We quickly learned to stop telling Saahil what our plans were, because he would take care of things before we could stop him. On our first full day, Saahil had taken off work, and with another friend from business school, Rahul, had driven us to India's ultimate tourist destination, the Taj Mahal. It was majestic beyond imagination, but on the way home, Saahil decided to show us another place that, to him, was just as impactful but in a different way. This was Vrindavan, a holy city and the birthplace of Krishna as well as the home to the Hare Krishna community.

Vrindavan was just off the highway running between Agra and Delhi, a small town nestled near a curve in the Yamuna River. When we pulled off the highway, we transitioned onto a smaller road running through fields with humble but sturdy cement-block houses dotting the way. The sun had started its evening descent when we arrived, and after a simple and delicious vegetarian meal at an ashram Saahil's grandfather had donated to, we headed into the town with the ashram manager as our guide. Saahil and Rahul wanted to show David and me two of the more known temples in town, particularly the Banke Bihari Temple.

The alley we were walking through now led to the temple, but what we hadn't realized before embarking was that no shoes are allowed within roughly a one-mile radius of the temple. We had been walking for a while when David and I noticed we had somehow been separated from our friends. Unsure of whether to stop or keep going, we decided to continue. The alley opened up to a bustling square where throngs of people poured into an unassuming but unmistakably important building. The sounds of chanting and traditional music emanated from the walls. This had to be the temple, and as we stared at its ancient stones, we felt hands grab our shoulders. Saahil and Rahul had found us, and with their hands on our backs, we were ushered into the temple with the rest of the swirling crowd.

The room inside was buzzing with a joyful and exuberant energy. About a hundred people were gathered in front of an ancient stage with a musty curtain. Just as we walked in, the curtain was pulled aside to reveal an amorphous rock mound. The moment the rock appeared, a commotion broke out. Chanting, symbols, and drumbeats filled the air, and everybody instantly dropped to the floor, splayed facedown in a prostrate prayer position. David and I were pushed down as well, and we found ourselves lying on the floor along with everyone else. Just as quickly, everybody sprang back up and repeated the whole operation: floor, arms extended, facedown, belly flat, then back up. In a daze, we were shepherded to a gathering of holy men at the side of the room to complete what we later learned was a traditional puja ritual. Somewhere in the shuffle, Saahil and Rahul had purchased traditional sweets, which we offered to the holy men. They gave us a soft milky treat in exchange, and we ate the sticky sweet mess with our fingers off small paper plates. The men placed wreaths of marigolds around our necks and gave us *tilakas*, smears of red sandalwood paste on our foreheads. The fragrant sandalwood smell was oddly mesmerizing. One of the men held my face in his warm, sandalwood-scented hands and mumbled a blessing I couldn't understand, but his eyes were smiling, and I smiled in return. We put our hands in prayer position and bowed to each other before our group rushed out the door just as quickly as we had entered. ***The whole exchange must have taken less than two minutes, but as we emerged from the din of the temple into the*** *comparably peaceful openness of the square outside, my mind went quiet.* It was like a deep hum was resonating through me, and I felt overcome with the most profound sense of peace I had ever known. I looked around me, and the light seemed different, almost rose-colored. It was as if the entire world was glowing.

The walk back down the alley felt completely different than the walk to the temple. The sights, sounds, and smells that had felt intimidating and overwhelming before now seemed gentle and welcoming. I clearly saw each face I passed, and I felt an undeniable sense of love for everyone and everything. *I love India.* The thought drifted into my mind, and the moment I heard the words, I knew they were true.

Our shoes were waiting right where we had left them when we reached the auto-rickshaw. We climbed into the vehicle, looking at one another with eyes glistening with tears. I was overcome with emotion, and the three men with me seemed to be as well. Saahil would later tell us he had never experienced that sort of rush of emotion in Vrindavan before, even though he had been there count-less times. As we drove away from the temple alley, a bright pink flower floated out of nowhere and landed on David's knee. Saahil gasped.

"Where did that flower come from?" he cried.

"It just came out of the sky," David said.

"This is a very good sign here in India," Saahil said. "A very good sign."

Saahil went on to explain that Vrindavan was a special place to visit. It was a place people in India came to at the beginning of new chapters and big changes in life. He looked at me, his eyes sincere, and said how remarkable it was for us to be here on the eve of my thirtieth birthday. We all fell silent, letting the proclamation sink in, and as we drove through the darkening town, I closed my eyes and sank into the powerful feelings of love and peace still coursing through my body. *There were those moments in life where things felt "meant to be," and this was one of them for me.* To be in Vrindavan not only just before a big birthday but also at the halfway point of the most life-changing adventure I had ever taken felt significant. I'm not a religious person, but on that evening, the ancient spirituality of Hindu traditions and the magic of India suffused my being. I had this feeling of attachment, like my heart would be forever bound to India from that night forward, and in that moment, I knew with utter certainty I would love our time there, that we would love our time there. I opened my eyes and looked at the faces of the people around me, those of my new love and my new friends. We all smiled and didn't stop smiling the entire way home.

CHAPTER 6

Finding Your Travel Rhythm

By the time you've been traveling for a couple months, you will most likely have found your stride. Like starting a new job, there is a point with travel when you grasp the basics and start to unlock the more nuanced elements that divide the professionals from the amateurs. Planning routes, finding accommodations, coordinating transport, getting your clothes washed, budgeting, and all the other mechanics of travel will feel like second nature. Your focus will start to shift more to the things that matter to you. This point, after the distractions of adjusting to travel life and before the end of the trip begins to loom, is the real sweet spot.

At this stage of our trip, we cared most about meeting people, eating and drinking amazing things, and finding local places unlike anything we could find at home. We are still stunned by how many amazing places we discovered, people we met, and memories we made in just a year. Although we loved our entire trip, there are particular moments that make us yearn to do it again. At the midpoint of our trip, we were focused on the present and pursuing the things we loved; it is hard to imagine anything better.

In this chapter, we share the techniques we learned to help us settle into our travel rhythm and focus on what mattered. We also share stories that bring to life how simple, intuitive, and happy life on the road can be and the unassuming moments that end up becoming some of the most beloved memories. This part of the trip is the joyful side of magic; it's the time to enjoy!

FINDING YOUR TRAVEL RHYTHM

And a Side of Sour Cream

Bucharest, Romania

DAVID

44.4268° N, 26.1025° E

Shaggy-hair, shabby clothes, svelte bodies and glowing—Alexandra and I had left India. Despite how much it pains me to say it, we looked a bit like the stereotypical young white couple who had found a new level of inner peace during their travels in India. We may not have found it in an ashram, and our thin bodies were more the result of excessive walking and food poisoning than vinyasa flows, but nuances aside, we fit the bill.

Whatever glow people back in the States would have perceived from us was lost on Romanians. Walking off the plane, I immediately felt a strong desire to toughen up, eat meat, and work out. I also realized I had never really mastered the art of *not* smiling, and Romania was a perfect place to practice. Although I technically had the physical advantage, with many men looking up at me, this was not the primary takeaway from our interactions. Hoping to learn a thing or two from Alexandra, who has Romanian roots and had been there before, I took some time to observe her. This was a terrible idea. Turns out that when Alexandra is not smiling, she looks like a little girl.

Although we were warmly greeted everywhere we went, Romanians would win in a global stare down—not by length of stare (India wins there), but rather by seriousness. Often from just a glance at another person, I would find myself asking soul-searching questions. Do I have what it takes to win in a fight? Am I in touch with life and death? Does my smiling make me less of a man? These were not questions I was accustomed to asking myself.

Our hosts in Romania were some of the most generous and upstanding people I have ever met. I immediately felt a great connection with them and looked forward to getting to know Marian, a non-blood uncle of Alexandra's who picked us up at the airport. He had a grand presence about him and spoke with great confidence and conviction. He took us to his beautiful home, and his wife, Adriana, greeted us warmly and made us feel immediately welcomed as honored guests despite our ragged image.

Within hours we were sitting on the patio of a stunning restaurant perfectly preserved from times long past. This restaurant was selected because we had requested local food for our first meal in Romania, and I could tell by Marian's eyes we were in for a treat. I had heard of a few classic dishes through an old Romanian friend in high school as well as from Alexandra's family, such as *mămăligă* (cornmeal porridge), *mititei* (fresh sausage), and *sarmale* (stuffed cabbage), but had yet to try any of them. I was exploding with joy and anticipation. *It is a rare and incredible opportunity to eat an almost entirely new cuisine.* The first dish to hit our table began a two-week food extravaganza. One meat-and-dairy-forward dish after the next was paired beautifully with local wine, beer, or hard alcohol.

It was comfort-food heaven. Every dish had round and generous flavors that gave a nod to what I might look like if I ate them for every meal. The seasoning made you feel nurtured and loved, as if the grandmother we all longed for growing up had prepared everything by hand. Cream was an acceptable topping for what seemed like every dish and was often presented in a sort of gravy bowl. Genius. Then there was the unfiltered beer. Maybe it was because I had grown accustomed to the very light and sweet beers in Asia, but Romanian unfiltered beer wowed me with its balanced flavors and creamy mouthfeel. The advertising tagline for Ursus, one of the larger brands in the country, even read "Probably the Best in the World," which at

the time I felt to be both reasonable and accurate. We were also quite taken by the local wine, which reminded us of Bordeaux and paired well with the richness of the food. Finally, there was the *țuică*, or *pálinka*, a potent liquor made from plums, peaches, or pears. Often homemade, its warming quality reminded you that you were alive, and within minutes of drinking it, all your worries seemed to melt away. It was glorious. The fact that *țuică* was often paired with small cubes of cured fat just took it to the next level for me.

The next morning, Marian generously tasked his assistant, Simona, with getting us some new clothes and haircuts. A quick look in the mirror removed any potential offense from the offer. After months on the road, we clearly needed the help. Alexandra and I did a quick Google search for men's haircuts and showed some options to Simona. She evaluated them, and in her charming accent, declared, "This one is sexy for you, and this one is sexy for the others." Turning to Alexandra, she asked, "Which would you like?" Romanians seem to have a talent for being direct. "Sexy for the others!" Alexandra said, an uncharacteristic but appropriate choice. By the end of the day, I gave it my best to make significant advancements toward embracing "sexy for the others": slicked-back hair, tight jeans, blue pleather jacket, and tan perforated leather shoes. Perhaps it was the fact I felt I needed to calm down my loud jacket or just the feeling in the air, but although I was having a splendid time, I did not smile in several photos that day. It was a first.

We spent the following two weeks traveling through the beautiful country of Romania, a country with a feeling all to itself. *The rich and unique culture, striking architecture, amazing food, and generous people were all things we would have totally missed had we based all our decisions on the destinations that guidebooks and blogs directed us toward.* Because of this experience, we evaluated future travel destinations in a new light. Countries like Georgia and Armenia floated to the top, whereas they might never have hit our radar before. In a country like Romania, it's also so much easier to escape the touristy stuff and fall into realness, where you're embraced as an individual rather than as part of a generic mass. If it had not been for Alexandra, Romania would not have been a country on my list, and I am so thankful for the experience.

SETTING YOUR PACE

It may take a little time to shake out, but when you get to the point when you know your travel-self better and what you are looking for, you'll really start to settle into your trip. Although there are no hard and fast rules, these guidelines are meant to help you get into the swing of things quicker.

1/ The Travel Day Cushion

Traveling from one place to another can be exhausting. Beyond just arriving in a new place, travel days involve packing and unpacking, transport to and from the bus, plane, train, or boat that will be taking you where you want to go, lots of negotiations, and often new languages or dialects as well as different currencies. It is exciting, but also requires lots of energy. What we found was that, more often than not, on travel days themselves we were so excited about getting to our next destination that we typically had enough energy to go out and explore on the first evening, but would feel pretty tired the *next* day. Take note of these trends and plan for them. We planned to do very little the day after we arrived in a new place, but we did plan to hit the town the night of. Knowing this gave us the liberty to chill out and get our bearings that second day without feeling badly about it. Find your own rhythm and embrace it; don't fight it.

2/ The Five-Day Recovery Rule

It's easy to get burned out when traveling. You might not have a lot of time in every destination, yet you can feel as if there are endless things to experience in each place you go. But if you don't structure your time well, you might end up too tired to really experience where you are. After a couple of times running ourselves into the ground, we created the "five-day recovery rule." Although seemingly obvious, this rule was invaluable. If we wanted to spend just two or three days in a place, we would go all out while there, then plan to have at least five days to recover at our next destination. For example, while in Ireland, we had a few jammed-packed days in Dublin and Galway followed by five days on the tranquil Aran Islands before traveling more. We had lots of energy for cities when we wanted to take advantage of them, while kicking back with a book in a pub or on a remote hillside felt glorious too. By following this intuitive rule, we were able to experience more and not worry about getting run-down.

3/ When Less Is More

As we progressed in our trip, we stopped seeing as many places and started seeing more of fewer places. We cut down our already trimmed list and saw less within each destination. That said, our time in those places got richer and richer. It took us a little while to get over the fear of missing out on things, but the benefit of getting to know a place far out-weighed our worries about not seeing enough. We learned to ignore impassioned statements like, "If you didn't see (enter amazing site here), then you were not really there. How did you not go?" We found that if we loved a place, we would stay. If we were not in love, we would leave.

continued ---→

4/ The Domino Effect

Following our passions never steered us wrong. When stating this so simply, we feel a bit obvious, but pursuing our interests unlocked not only a route we loved but also facilitated so many of our favorite moments throughout the trip. Our passions were like a compass, pointing us in the right directions and steering us down winding trails of happy discovery with joyful moments knocking into one another like dominos. Our taste buds often set the dominos in motion, with one good meal leading to many more, or a seemingly simple cup of coffee opening the door to a whole world of local favorites. Not surprisingly, the places we gravitated toward were often filled with other people like ourselves who shared interests similar to ours. Over a cup of coffee or an afternoon drink, we would find opportunities to chat up a friendly face at the neighboring table or barstool, and when we expressed genuine interest in trying *their* favorite restaurants, visiting *their* favorite areas, locals would happily open up and share their beloved haunts. These conversations became the perfect launching point for stumbling upon other things we loved: fantastic hidden gems of restaurants, cool homegrown shops gloriously free of the clutter marketed to tourists, hip and up-and-coming neighborhoods frequently not talked about in the main guidebooks, and good live-music scenes. Every time we followed the dominos, so to speak, we felt the delicious thrill of serendipitous discovery, the joy of stumbling upon one great spot after another.

TRAVELING WITH DIETARY RESTRICTIONS

Alexandra

One of the most glorious parts of our trip was all the different foods we enjoyed. We savored the variety of flavors we encountered across the globe. Eating the local cuisine really helps you get to know a place better and experience it all the more deeply, but if you have a dietary restriction or food allergy, being able to fully enjoy your meals can be a bit of a challenge, particularly in countries where English isn't widely spoken or understood.

I have celiac disease, and a lot of people asked me how it was to travel with such a challenging food condition. Surprisingly, navigating gluten-free options in the rest of the world proved to be far easier than it was in the U.S. as a whole, and I only got sick a handful of times. What's more, countries we assumed would be super difficult for me, like Italy and Ireland, proved to be some of the most gluten-free-friendly places I have ever been to.

Communicating an allergy or dietary restriction can certainly be a challenge, but there are a few tricks to help with this. You can look up and memorize the words or phrases for your allergy or food preferences with the help of an online translator, but better than that, you can ask a kind stranger who speaks English to write an explanatory note for you in the native language of the place you're visiting. I did this throughout Southeast Asia and in Japan, and whenever we would go to a restaurant, I would politely show our server or cook the note. This worked without fail each and every time.

It's important to remember to be as respectful as possible when explaining your dietary restriction or food allergy, though, particularly in countries like Japan and France, where a lot of pride is taken in the cuisine. Be humble, appreciative, and understanding, and you will likely receive the same treatment in return.

August Holiday

Lyon, France

ALEXANDRA

45.7640° N, 4.8357° E

August. It felt as though all of France had gone on holiday, probably because most people had. Cities had emptied. Streets had grown quiet. Shops and restaurants had put up signs reading *fermé pour les vacances* (closed for vacation), shuttering their windows and locking their doors for anywhere from two to four weeks. Parking was plentiful. Tourists continued to descend upon Paris, and a selection of restaurants catering to this crowd remained open, along with museums and other sightseeing destinations. The locals, in the meanwhile, had flocked to the seaside, quiet mountain villages, and temperate islands for their annual holiday pilgrimage. It was a beautiful ritual to behold.

David and I arrived in Lyon mere days before the August holiday season officially commenced. Having spent the last week touring the wine regions of the Loire Valley, we felt compelled to dive deeper and explore Burgundy. We had found a charming flat to rent in La Croix-Rousse, a hilly neighborhood with an artistic spirit unique from the rest of the city. The neighborhood's architecture harkens back to Lyon's heritage in the silk industry, with most of the buildings featuring large vaulted ceilings with exposed wooden rafters. Our flat showcased these signature ceilings along with tall windows that allowed golden summer light to pour into the rooms. The woman who owned the flat seemed to share interests similar to ours. We were thrilled to find a turntable and an excellent collection of records. The kitchen was small but highly functional. We had rented the flat for ten days in order to have lots of time to explore the surrounding wine region.

We woke up on our first morning ready to find a café, a rental car, and a list of the must-visit wineries. After all, this was France, and Burgundy was right up the road. How could we not go? We began to walk the neighborhood in search of a good café, but most were already closed. We finally found a place with the unpromising name La Zebra and décor straight out of an '80s music video. The coffee was fine. We began to research wineries and rental cars, which was when all the roadblocks began to appear. First, the rental-car rates were astronomical due to everyone wanting to snatch them up for their own vacations. Second, the chances of wineries even being open were looking slim. Like the businesses in town, the wineries also closed for a few weeks during August—a fact we had overlooked. Sitting in the subpar café, we felt we would either get the dregs of Lyon or the dregs of the wineries. What had we done? We spent the afternoon sulking and feeling trapped. We didn't want to go to the seaside with everyone else, but we didn't want to feel like we were wasting our precious time.

One of the only restaurants still open in the neighborhood was a new café named L'Oenothèque de Lyon. Since they had just opened a few weeks prior to the August holiday season, the brother owners had to remain open in order to offset some of the costs of launching the business. We thought we would cook at home most nights, but after our disappointing day, we wanted a night out. We strolled to the café and investigated the menu. It was small and simple. There were a handful of starters, beef tartare, and steak frites. Two desserts rounded things out along with a gorgeous wine selection. We settled in at one of the patio tables and ordered sautéed shrimp, the tartare, and steak frites. While David can eat raw meat every day, I'm a bit more selective, but this tartar was the most memorable either of us had ever had. The meat was minced to perfection, soft and supple, and it was mixed with mustard and briny bits of pickles. During the meal, we met a friendly woman who was comfortably eating by herself. It turned out she was the girlfriend of one of the owners. *As we talked, the colors of our situation began to change.* We realized we had been talking about how much we had been craving some downtime, time to do nothing but write, read, play music, and enjoy. We had resisted this desire because of the temptations of all the amazingness everywhere we went, but perhaps the August holiday was the perfect excuse to do what we really wanted to do.

We quickly fell into a blissful rhythm of waking to the mid-morning sun filtering in through the gauzy curtains and making coffee on the stove top. On Sunday morning there was one of those emblematic French markets. Food stalls, produce stands, cheese mongers, butchers, rotisseries, and more stretched for blocks, and we lost ourselves in the magical wonder of the incredible bounty of fruits, vegetables, cured meats, cheeses, yogurts, and perfectly roasted chickens. Like everyone else, we bought a rotisserie chicken to eat for a late lunch along with a simple salad and array of cheeses, some soft and delicate and others strong, pungent triple creams you had to scoop onto your bread with a spoon. At the market, David discovered a patisserie that sold the most enormous meringues we had ever seen. Bigger than my head, the meringues came plain or dipped in dark chocolate. We opted for the dark chocolate version and made the glorious mistake of eating the entire thing in one sitting. We found the most indulgent vanilla yogurt with cream on top. It had flecks of vanilla bean, and the blue ceramic containers were so charming we saved four to bring home as coffee cups.

We also began to recognize the locals' daily rituals and adopted a few ourselves. David would stroll to a bakery at 5:00 p.m. for an evening baguette. We befriended the cheese monger at the local shop, and for the days leading up until her holiday closure, we would stop in and sample something new, always leaving with at least three different cheeses to enjoy as an afternoon snack or after-dinner treat.

We spent our afternoons savoring the slowness of the days. David wrote songs on the little Martin travel guitar we had carried around the world with us, and I devoured book after book from our host's English-friendly collection. Rosé replaced water. At sunset we would stroll to the nearby park and settle in for an *aperitif,* opening a bottle of wine and unwrapping the most perfect dome of goat cheese while watching the sunset. Sometimes David would bring the guitar, and we would dip into our own little world, playing and singing together as the light dimmed. We were in heaven.

We ended up going back to L'Oenothèque de Lyon two more times before we left the city. Both times, the lovely woman we had met on that first night was there, and soon we were friendly with not only her but the owners as well. On our last visit to the restaurant, she and the brothers invited us in at the end of our meal for a farewell glass of Champagne. We both remarked on how wonderful we thought the wine was, and when the brothers showed us the bottle, we took a picture to remember it by. When we got back to the flat that night, we were still talking about how delicious the Champagne had been. David looked up the bottle online, and we both gasped when we read it was a €120 bottle. What a luxury!

During our time in Lyon, we also took advantage of the city bike share. We would rent bikes and cruise to the bottom of the hill where the more commercial part of the city was. Some shops remained open, and we would bike along streets lined with galleries, fashionable boutiques, and artisanal-food purveyors. One afternoon we bought a bottle of wine and biked to the banks of the Rhône River, where David

jury-rigged two wine glasses with an Opinel knife and plastic water bottle. I've rarely seen him more proud.

The bike ride back up the hill to La Croix-Rousse was quite the workout. Even with all the walking we had been doing, I felt a bit out of shape. David has what his cycling buddies like to call "old man strength." No matter how in or out of shape he is, he's able to chew up hills with fortitude. I don't share this ability. One evening, we were making our attempt to conquer some streets that crisscross up the hill. David was in the lead, and I puffed along behind him. Sweat poured down my back and face. As we rounded the second to last turn, we passed a café we had biked by several times in the last few days. Normally the café was closed, but tonight it was open. Inviting golden light streamed onto the small terrace, and contented patrons laughed over glasses of wine and plates of food. A few people even cheered us on as we labored past on our bicycles, shouting words of encouragement and raising their glasses. Even in our pain, we were able to take note of how blissful the scene looked, so as soon as we had parked our bikes at the top of the hill, we shook off the sweat and walked the two streets back down.

The café was named Au Temps Perdu. The owner welcomed us warmly and seated us at a comfortable table in a romantic corner. The small menu was scrawled on a chalkboard, which the waiter held up for us to read. He provided some input on some of the items we weren't as familiar with and made a few recommendations, many of which we took. Although we were hungry from the ride, we were still tremendously hot, so we ordered a large salad resplendent with prosciutto, cheese, and seasonal produce, and a plate of succulent prawns swimming in an herbaceous garlic sauce. Paired with glasses of bright white wine, the food was spectacular. We ended the meal with a perfectly browned crème brûlée.

As we savored the last few bites of our dessert, we reveled in the atmosphere of the café. We observed the other diners, all of whom seemed familiar with one another. The owner moved back and forth from the kitchen to the dining room, playfully interacting with the guests and helping out with the cooking. The waiter was both server and bartender. We noticed a classical guitar leaning against one wall. After we had finished our meal, David asked if he could play. The owner was delighted and immediately brought over the guitar. David began to play a Spanish melody, and one of the couples sitting nearby got up to dance. It all felt very French.

When we left for the night, the owner encouraged us to come back again. We only had a few days left in Lyon, but the very next night we found ourselves back at Au Temps Perdu. The atmosphere had such a magnetic pull on us. That second night our meal wasn't quite as magnificent, but it was equally if not more memorable. We made the risky move of ordering very local dishes: frogs' legs and *andouillette*. The former was more straightforward, but the latter ended up being quite the surprise. I had ordered *andouillette* under the assumption it was a sausage, but it turned out to be a tripe casserole. Having made this discovery, I could barely stomach the dish. I gave it to David, who said he didn't mind it, but his appetite changed when I asked, "Can you taste the poop?" while he was mid-bite. David's meal must have involved the deaths of roughly twenty frogs. The plate was piled with legs upon legs upon legs. He was able to get through half, then struggled through the last quarter out of sheer guilt over how many frogs must have died.

As we lingered over our meal, the restaurant began to fill with a small crowd of locals. Some we recognized from the night before, including the dancing couple. We felt as if we had happened upon a little party and watched happily from the corner as they opened bottles of Champagne and began pulling out instruments. There were two guitars, a tambourine, and a maraca-like thing that made a rainy shimmer when shaken. We were invited to join the group, and

as more glasses of Champagne were poured, the owner went to the front of the restaurant and pulled down the metal grate, closing us all in for the evening. It was at that point that the cigarette smoking began with flagrant disregard for the government-issued *Ne Pas Fumer* (no smoking) signs hanging on the walls. The room filled with laughter and the sounds of classic French songs from the '60s. One man in the group sounded like a French Bruce Springsteen. David was given a guitar and joined in the revelry, and I sang on a few songs as well. At one point, a woman even pulled out a cello from who knows where. We had somehow stumbled into another time or a scene from a classic French film. We stayed until three in the morning, playing music, drinking wine, smoking cigarettes, and getting to know the crew. It was one of the best nights of the trip, and for an evening, we let ourselves get utterly lost in the underbelly of late-night French café life. As we walked back to our flat, holding each other and strolling through the empty streets, we were filled with smiles. What a night! What a city! We felt at home and never wanted to leave.

We often think about how none of this would have happened if we hadn't come to Lyon during the start of the August holiday season. What others might have considered the worst time to visit a French city, we ultimately considered the best. *We found life, real life, in the in-between.* Of all the places to not feel like a tourist, we definitely didn't expect it to be in France.

CHAPTER 7

People Make All the Difference

Vacationers and travelers are received quite differently. We were skeptical of the stories we had heard of how open and generous people could be to travelers. It seemed a bit far-fetched, especially since we were not college-aged backpackers looking to crash wherever. The idea that adults we hardly knew would offer up their homes and food or take the time to provide a mini-tour seemed improbable at best. Perhaps we even believed that mistrust came with age.

What we see now is that there is a fundamental difference between welcoming a vacationer into your home or town and welcoming a traveler. Generally speaking, vacationers are looking for a respite from their often stressful and hectic lives. Their focus is on being taken away and rejuvenated in a new place. Travelers, on the other hand, are looking to learn and experience as much as possible about where they are. They are not looking to escape or seeking a reprieve. We often sensed from locals that a part of them was thinking, *Out of all the places in the world to visit, you chose here. I want you to know my home and its people are as good or better than any in the world!* Having us leave with a real understanding of their home seemed as much a point of personal pride as it did anything else. Learning this comparative context and the difference between a traveler and a vacationer revealed the larger picture of why people were so willing to show us a great time. Our experience was a reflection of their individual kindnesses, the pride they took in their heritage, and the opportunity to have their home compete with great places all around the world. We often felt this more intensely in small towns, but even in big cities people wanted to show us the real side of their city as opposed to the guidebook version.

In this chapter, we illuminate the special inherent connectivity that travel infuses in relationships, both new and old. We share stories of reconnection with old friends and moments of instant connection with new ones. Travel friendships are a special breed. The new relationships we forged and the old relationships we rekindled were some of the most rewarding elements of our journey. When we look back on our trip now, we not only think about all the incredible places we saw, the things we did, and the cultures we experienced, but we also think about the people we visited and the moments we shared together.

A GLOBAL VIEW OF FRIENDS AND FAMILY

Before we left on our trip, we mapped out all the countries and cities where we had friends and family. We were shocked at the number. Between the two of us, we knew people all over the world, and through the connections of friends-of-friends, family friends, and new people we met on the way, that people-to-visit count increased all the more. Having people to visit gave us reasons to see places we ended up loving that may not have otherwise made the list, and as we've mentioned before, having a local guide show you around is invaluable.

Before you set off on your journey, sit down and make a list of the people you know living abroad. You may be surprised at the number of global connections you have, and there is an unbelievable joy in reconnecting with a friend or family member you haven't seen in years.

CONNECTIONS

1. **New Zealand**
   family friend we hadn't seen in fifteen years

2. **New South Wales, Australia**
   new acquaintance through family friend

3. **Singapore**
   distant relative

4. **Osaka, Japan**
   former classmate we hadn't seen in five years

5. **Tokyo, Japan**
   new acquaintance through friend back home; new acquaintance through distant cousin

6. **New Delhi, India**
   former classmates we hadn't seen in five years

7. **Bangalore, India**
   new acquaintances through former boss from back home

8. **Bucharest, Romania**
   close family friends

9. **Prague, Czech Republic**
   former classmate we hadn't seen in five years

10. **Dublin, Ireland**
    acquaintance we met while traveling in India

11. **Milltown Malbay, Ireland**
    distant relative

12. **London, England**
    former boss; former classmates we hadn't seen in five-plus years

13. **Leeds, England**
    new friend we made while traveling in Thailand

14. **Edinburgh, Scotland**
    new friends we made while traveling in India

15. **Paris, France**
    new acquaintance through friend back home; family friend we hadn't seen in ten-plus years

16. **Tours, France**
    friend we hadn't seen in ten years

17. **Köln, Germany**
    family friends we hadn't seen in five years

18. **Mannheim, Germany**
    new friends we made while traveling in Thailand

19. **Hamburg, Germany**
    new friend we made while traveling in Cambodia

20. **Berlin, Germany**
    friend we hadn't seen in ten years

21. **Grasse, France**
    parents of former classmate we had only met once before

22. **Nice, France**
    new friend we made while eating out in Tours, France

23. **Rome, Italy**
    new acquaintance through family back home

24. **Florence, Italy**
    new acquaintance through friend we met while traveling in Thailand

25. **Bologna, Italy**
    new friend we made while traveling in Thailand

26. **Milan, Italy**
    distant relative; relatives of friends back home

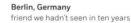

The Irish Cousins

Milltown Malbay, Ireland

ALEXANDRA

52.8562° N, 9.4008° W

Nell and Jim Gleason are as Irish as Irish come. They have six kids, including a set of twins, own and maintain a farm, and, until recently, managed a general store and traditional Irish music pub. When the local church was under construction for renovations, Nell and Jim opened their pub to the town for Sunday service and a convenient transition to postworship libations. Nell had also run a book club with her friends for over forty years, and her personal library was beyond impressive. She had somehow read countless novels in between raising a family, working a farm, and running a pub and store. When we were telling the Gleasons about our trip, Nell kindly commented, "Well, I have no idea what that's like. We never took a day of vacation."

Nell and Jim are David's somewhat distant cousins, with whom he did not have regular contact, but they had generously invited us to stay in their home in Milltown Malbay for a few nights during our time in Ireland. We had just come from five days on the tranquil bliss of Inis Meáin, the most remote of the three Aran Islands off the coast of Galway, and we were over the moon to discover that our stay with Nell and Jim coincided with the Willie Clancy Festival, the biggest traditional Irish music festival, which took place annually in midsummer in Milltown Malbay. Irish musicians of all ages had descended upon the town, and for the next few days and nights, every single pub in the center of town (and there were a shocking number considering how small the town was), would be filled with the sometimes uplifting but often heartbreaking sounds of traditional Irish music from midmorning until well after dark. We couldn't believe our luck.

When we arrived, Nell let us know the festival officially began the next day, but there would be some more casual gatherings at a few of the pubs in town that evening. She suggested we go, but not until we had eaten our fill at dinner. The definition of the gracious hostess, Nell prepared an Irish feast for us on our first evening: lamb, potatoes, cabbage, soda bread, and plenty of creamy and golden Irish butter. Nell piled David's plate as high as if he were a laborer in her field needing to refuel after a long day's work. David enthusiastically polished off his plate, but little did he know he was accepting a quiet invitation to a three-day eating challenge. For the next two mornings, Nell steadily increased the amount of food on David's plate, beginning with four rashers of bacon, two sausages, three eggs, and a half loaf of bread to a whopping six rashers of bacon, four sausages, two slices of blood pudding, four eggs, and a half loaf of bread. David managed with the first breakfast, but after over an hour of happily struggling through breakfast two, he had to admit defeat. Overfeeding was clearly a sign of love in Ireland, and in this household, the

stove did not have an "off" button. There was always a full kettle on ready to make someone a cup of tea, and Nell ran a microbakery of sorts, with loaves of hot bread fresh from the oven every day. It all felt like magic.

After dinner, we retired to the sitting room, where it was apparently a family tradition to play music and sing after supper. I could feel my palms break out in a sweat. David was handed a guitar, and Derek, Nell and Jim's middle child and one of only a few *uilleann* pipe makers in the world, took up a set of pipes to play. He kicked off the performances, playing an achingly beautiful traditional tune. When he was done, Nell turned to me and inquired about my musical skills. I weakly replied, "I sing."

"Oh, lovely," Nell said, beaming. "Sing us a song, then."

I desperately grasped for some song I both knew by heart and could comfortably sing a capella in front of a small group, but my mind betrayed me by going blank. Somewhere from behind the cobwebs emerged a tune that had been my fallback at every single audition I had done over the years, and without thinking further, I began belting out "Part of Your World" from Disney's *The Little Mermaid* with as much heart and gusto as I could muster. When I finished, I looked over at David, who was trying to keep from laughing. I glanced about the room at the perplexed expressions of his family members, who had been trying to follow the lyrics, as most Irish songs tell quite the story. My mermaid tale had clearly not moved them.

"Well," Nell said. "You have a lovely voice."

David was next in line, and he dove headlong into an energetic performance of Bob Dylan's "You're No Good," practically yelling the lyrics at his now completely shocked cousins. Our musical choices had definitely deviated from the norm. When David strummed the last note, Nell let out a gasp and said, "Well, now, that was quite spirited!" I think they had had enough because there was no request for seconds, and it wasn't long before Nell suggested we head into town to get to the pubs in time to grab a drink and a seat before the (real) music started.

Nell and Jim lived a short ten-minute drive outside the main town, although for me it was a harrowing stretch. Driving in Ireland is like an extreme sport. The roads are beyond narrow and lined with stone walls that are sheathed in lush bushels of grass in the summer months. To my innocent and untrained eye, the roads all appeared to be one lane, but David had experience driving in Ireland from a family trip years earlier, so he was in on the secret that these roads accommodated two-lane traffic, including the not-so-occasional tour bus. Some deeply seated force of heritage took over David's body and soul in Ireland, from his ability to drink Guinness and whiskey like the best of them to his astonishing capabilities at maneuvering these death-defying roads. On our drive into town that night, I alternated between covering my eyes, gripping the door handle, and flat-out screaming as David shot through the windy lanes, grass brushing the sides of our car and warning of the stony collision just beyond its outer reaches.

Despite all my fears and doubts, we made it to town in one piece and found a parking spot not far from the main drag. The first pub we came across had such a friendly and welcoming vibe that we couldn't resist going in. Several musicians were warming up in the corner, and the bar was comfortably crowded. A jovial energy filled the air, and we drank it in as eagerly as we did the beverages the bartender set down before us. Soon after first arriving in Ireland, I discovered that casual bar conversation, or "having a crack," was a favorite pastime, so I wasn't surprised when the gentleman next to David dove in for a chat. The man was a musician who had grown up in Milltown Malbay and was in town for the festival. His eclectic style brought to mind images of Bono and Keith Richards, and he played in a rock band heavily inspired by Tom Waits, Leonard Cohen, and Nick Cave. Once their musical compatibility had been established, he and David became instant friends, and as they talked, the man's face suddenly lit up.

"Wait!" he exclaimed. "You're the Gleasons' cousins! The American cousins!"

"How did you know that?" David asked, bemused.

"Everyone in town knows that!" the man laughed.

Soon we were being introduced as the Gleasons' American cousins to a whole host of people at the bar, and as the night went on, we had made friends with almost everyone in the pub—faces we would continue to see throughout the next two evenings at performances across the town. ***We were so far away from home, but because we were family, we were in, welcomed into the fold and treated like long-lost friends.*** We spent the night chatting and drinking, surrounded by the loving embrace of the lively sounds of the Irish tunes being played around us. As the hours went on, we eventually reached the point in the night when the owner of the pub "locks" everyone in. The door is closed and bolted so no one else can get in from outside. It signifies last call, which in Ireland means you order as many beers as possible that can fit on any available flat surface as well as the start of some of the best music you'll hear in a night. As we all settled in with our final drinks, a middle-aged woman sitting at our table stood up, and a hush descended upon the room. Without any introduction or to-do, she began to sing a hauntingly beautiful and heart-achingly tragic Irish song. Tears stung at the backs of my eyes, and it was as if the entire room held its breath while she sang. When she finished, a resounding applause broke the respectful silence. She smiled and made a joke before taking her seat again and opening the floor up to the next willing party. The night went on in this fashion, a show-and-tell of musical abilities similar to what we had experienced back at Nell and Jim's home after dinner but at a much grander scale. *If this is being Irish,* I thought, *count me in.*

REACHING OUT TO YOUR NETWORK

Staying with a local brings so many benefits to your travel experience, but asking someone if you can stay with him or her, even a good friend with whom you have regular contact, can be a delicate dance. Having houseguests, no matter how fun, is still work for the host, so it's helpful to approach the request appreciatively and with flexibility. We found the following tips to be useful throughout our travels with a range of different hosts, from long-lost friends and former classmates to new acquaintances and distant relatives.

TIP 1: ▶ Put the ball in their court. When reaching out to potential hosts, start the conversation by letting them know you'll be coming through their part of the world. If they are up for hosting you, they will usually suggest it without your having to ask, and if they aren't up for it, you'll be able to avoid an awkward moment. In our experience, we never had to ask to stay with any of the people we connected with, no matter how well or little we knew them. Most everyone we approached extended an invitation, and we were delighted to accept.

TIP 2: ▶ Know your limits. More often than not, the depth with which you know someone will determine how long you're able to stay with him or her, although sometimes there are exceptions to this rule. In general, though, the better you know someone, the longer you can stay with him or her. Similarly to

continued ▶━▶

the initial invitation to stay, we often left the length of the stay in the hands of the host, but in cases where we asked about a specific amount of time, we would suggest the dates with a very strong caveat that if they didn't work for the host, we were more than fine.

TIP 3: ▶ Always have a gift. It's incredibly generous of people to host you, so always make sure to have something you can give them in thanks. Gifts can range from the material to the experiential. While traveling in Southeast Asia and India, we picked up a few light-weight handcrafted items at markets and brought these with us as fun gifts from our travels to give to future hosts. The most common gift we gave, though, was a home-cooked meal. Even if you're on a budget and traveling with a small bag, you can go out and get some fresh ingredients and a good bottle of wine, depending on where you are. We would always ask our hosts first, since this gift involved using their kitchens, but people were excited to be cooked for. We got really good at making roast chicken, and this became a classic for us as we traveled from place to place. This gift was a nice way to show our appreciation while also being able to have one last shared experience together during our visit.

KEEPING AN OPEN MIND

It sounds so simple, but keeping an open mind about who you meet on the road can really unlock some of the most incredible moments. Throughout your journey, you'll encounter people from all walks of life and of different ages and stages, and it's remarkable what can happen when you put aside any preconceived notions or assumptions in your interactions. One evening in Tours, France, we stumbled upon an Indian restaurant. Intrigued and perhaps a bit nostalgic, we decided to see what a French take on Indian cuisine would be. We ended up sitting next to an adorable older couple and struck up a conversation with them. Our talk soon turned to India. They had a trip coming up, and the memory of ours was still fresh in our minds. As our respective meals drew to a close, the woman invited us to come see her when we were in Nice, her hometown, in a few weeks' time. We took her up on her offer and ended up having one of the most memorable days of the trip. It turned out she was a professional tour guide, and she took us on a private tour of the famous artist Jean Cocteau's home, then brought us back to her flat for a delicious home-cooked meal. On the surface, we were so different from this woman and where she was in life, but the connection that unfolded couldn't have been more effortless. This is all part of the magic of meeting new people while on the road.

THE PEOPLE YOU'LL SEE

As you may expect, travel is an amazing opportunity to visit family, reconnect with old friends, and get to know friends of friends. People we had not seen since college, or who were loose connections to people we knew at home, opened their doors to us, providing us with not only places to stay but also enthusiastic tours of their cities. We were aided by dozens of people with links to back home, and folks we had not considered as connections before leaving became gracious hosts and good friends.

Another remarkable surprise was how close we became to a handful of other travelers. We had always expected to meet people and make new friends, but we didn't understand how enduring those new friendships would be. The combination of abundant time, incredible shared experiences, and similar perspectives on life set up a very good formula for building amazing bonds. In the travel environment, relationships often get deeper faster, and it is far from uncommon to end up traveling with new people you meet in multiple destinations. Before leaving we would never have expected to make sustaining relationships on the road. But now we have several friends we met while traveling that we keep in regular contact with. We have even vacationed with a few, and many came to our wedding after we got back home.

Meals That Last a Lifetime

Tours, France

DAVID

47.3941° N, 0.6848° E

There are meals that last a lifetime.

For ten years I had been anticipating visiting my great friend Kevin in Tours, France. I had shared a flat with him and other students for six months while living in Cape Town, South Africa. I deeply cherish the memories we made then. They constantly remind me that life is for the living, to take some risks, listen to your gut, and not fear going big.

Kevin, our friend Aaron, and I were a team, and we lived like we would never live again. We drove an old original Mini bought from a pawnshop that overheated most every time we took it out. It had terrible brakes that often made us scream in terror as we barreled uncontrollably down the hillsides of Cape Town. The term "emergency brake" still holds special meaning as I recall pulling that thing with all the strength my wiry arms could muster in order to slow the old car down. But functioning brakes or not, we drove like hell all over that city, country, and even a few neighboring nations. When I think back, some integral part of me remains connected to the rich and exuberant energy that thrives within this special part of Africa and the joyful times Kevin and Aaron and I had there. It was the best life I had ever known.

Since the moment I waved goodbye to Kevin before boarding the plane to the moment he picked us up from the train in Tours a decade later, we did not speak a word to each other. Maybe it was that I spoke no French and Kevin's English was less than stellar, or maybe it was because we were dudes. *Yet when we saw each other again, there were no apologies for our lack of communication, and we instantaneously picked up where we left off.* It seemed to me that we had an understanding that we were both fulfilling our promises to each other: mine that I would someday make it out to France and his that he would show me his family's pride and joy—their restaurant.

Making my way with Alexandra to the family's restaurant, La Roche Le Roy, filled me with a sense of satisfaction far beyond any expectation. The feeling surpassed some of my greatest moments of personal achievement. Walking under the limestone archway leading to the dimly lit entrance, I could barely keep up. I was quietly overwhelmed. I was reunited with a true friend, and there was a palpable feeling of pride between us. Upon arrival, Kevin left no doubt about his anticipation and happiness to see us. He gave us his car and moved himself, his pregnant wife, and their three-year-old son to his in-laws' house in order to give us his apartment stocked with the loveliest rosé. And now, he was giving us the very long-awaited meal he had promised so many years ago.

We were warmly greeted by his mother, who ran the front of house, and seated outside at an elegant patio with red tablecloths, wooden chairs with velvet cushions, and calming lighting. The temperature was cool and comfortable on that July evening. Alexandra and I both felt like highly honored guests, and at the same time, part of the family that had created this beautiful restaurant. You could see and feel the hard work and dedication Kevin's family had poured into every single detail, earning a much-deserved Michelin star for twenty-six consecutive years. Kevin explained that the building was once a royal hunting lodge. It looked to us more like a small castle with its spiraling towers of silvery limestone, sumptuous rooms, massive fireplace, and great sense of old-world riches. He also explained that it was good that we came when we did, because they were soon going to sell.

Everything was waiting for us, even gluten-free bread the bakers had perfected especially for Alexandra. I will never forget the deep sense of blissful arrival I had while eating each phenomenal course and drinking the wine pairings. We started the meal with Champagne, and each delicious dish effortlessly flowed into the next: chilled tomato soup introduced a bouquet of asparagus topped with bacon and a soft-boiled egg. Although the menu was set, we were asked to choose a main course. Kevin and I went with the more adventurous option: a classic French dish of sweetbreads and morels cooked in a pastry crust, while Alexandra had a filet of fish with crispy skin, topped with chanterelles and little nuggets of pancetta. The meal was impeccable. It expressed the rich simplicity of the French countryside and the refined elegance of something well practiced. *The experience may never be topped;* I was reunited with a friend as well as with some of my fondest memories, over a perfect meal that was promised to me during a time that began to feel like an abandoned dream.

As with all dreams, it is hard to convey the import of this one, but the night will stand as a marker in my life: a reminder to live big, trust in my gut, invest in good people, and never let fear get in the way of life.

SECTION III

COMING BACK HOME

CHAPTER 8

Preparing to Make a Soft Landing

The last few weeks of your trip are a unique time. At this point, the nomadic day-to-day existence that might have seemed foreign and unfamiliar months ago has become the new normal, and traveling is a second-nature way of experiencing the world. For us, each day felt full and engaging, but our return flights to the States loomed bigger and bigger on the horizon.

It is difficult to determine how you may feel about coming home. Some people we met on the road were looking forward to getting back to friends, family, and life back home, while others found ways to extend the magical life of travel. If you choose to lengthen your trip, it does not mean that your life goes on pause. One friend, for example, spent three years making his way back home, but when he finally did land on native soil, he brought with him a world of experience and a traveling companion who later became his wife. Take a moment during these last few months to evaluate if your return plan is still what is best for you. At the time, we felt our budget would not have allowed for more time traveling, but looking back we could have figured something out. If travel is still what you want, there are lots of ways to make it work.

Choosing to go home brings with it a suite of potential feelings, just as departing does. It is important to listen to what you feel during this time, as very often these feelings can provide great insight on your life and future choices. In this chapter, we touch on what it felt like for us to know home was not too far away, and some of the issues that cropped up as a result.

TO RE-ENGAGE OR NOT TO RE-ENGAGE

Alexandra

When we left on the trip, David and I made a commitment not to engage with work until we got back. For most of the trip, we stood by this decision. Work could wait until we got back, and we had the additional cushion of the savings we had set aside for our return. But when we had about three months left in the trip, I became tempted by a few emails from old employers and recruiters inquiring about my availability upon return. Not realizing how much it would affect me, I thought it would be wise to pursue a couple options in preparation for our return. This was a terrible mistake. Without my realizing it, my focus began to shift, and I quickly disengaged from the trip. Although I was completely unaware of it in the moment, thinking about home and work made me want to pull off the Band-Aid of going back home and dive right in. Rather than thinking about the incredible places we were in and engaging with David and the people we were meeting, I mentally flew away, stressing about returning to my career and preparing for potential interviews I would take from the road. Before I knew it, I had a Skype interview set up, and David and I were no longer emotionally traveling together.

I eventually came to my senses and returned from this hiatus, but it took over a month and is my single biggest regret of our trip. I spoke to other travelers our age, and many of them went through similar experiences, especially if they didn't have a job lined up for when they got home. Although you may be able to remain engaged in your trip while re-engaging with work back home, if you choose to do so, I encourage you to consider the risks.

There was a plus side to all this, though, which is that the entire experience illuminated for me how incredible it was to be engaged in travel. Never before had I ever been so present and engaged as I was on the road. I still vividly remember simple moments of walking down streets and taking in the beauty and uniqueness of the architecture around me, the colors, the people, the feeling in the air, and even simple everyday things like advertisements, street signs, and graffiti. This is a perspective and level of awareness I treasure and work hard to bring forward in my life today.

MAKING THE MOST OF
THE LAST COUPLE MONTHS

There will come a point on your trip when you pass the "equinox," and you know the time left is shorter than the time you've been away. When the balance has shifted like this, the temptation to start re-engaging with life back home can be strong, but it's important to remember the remaining weeks you have left are still significant and likely longer than any trip you may take again . . . at least for a while. These tips can help you stay totally engaged and really enjoy what may be some of the sweetest parts of your travels.

1/ Embrace the Value of Letting Go
After traveling for a while, you'll have likely learned how to let go, be present, and simply enjoy. Take note of your newfound ability to do this as an adult who already knows what it's like to have mounting responsibilities. Use this time to think about how to incorporate this valuable lesson into the life you'll live back home and maintain this perspective as you move forward.

2/ Remember Life Is Short
At this point in your trip, you'll have a pretty solid sense of what your budget is: how much you've spent, what you have left, and your spending patterns. There is no prize for coming home under budget, so this final stretch is a great time to spend what you have, or even give yourself a bit more of a cushion if you can. It's also the perfect moment to pick up a few gifts for

continued ▸──

yourself. Having objects and tokens from your journey in your home will be lovely little reminders of memories from the road.

3/ Consider Travel Buddies

Invite people to meet you on the road. Having friends and family come and travel with you can help you start to reconnect with life back home without going too deep. It's also a great way to bring people along on your journey and create some stories together.

4/ Have a Grand Finale

Saving one of your "must do" experiences or planning something special for the final weeks of your trip can help keep the energy positive and your mind engaged on the present. Plus, it always feels good to end on a high note!

Roma!

Rome, Italy

ALEXANDRA

41.9028° N, 12.4964° E

Rome.

The ancient city. The city of romance. The city of thieves. The city of food and hectic traffic and espresso bars brimming with people talking loudly and gesturing even more loudly.

We arrived with a thrumming sense of anticipation. I had been to Rome before but not since I was fourteen, and David had been busy dreaming of Rome for years. We had just shy of three weeks left in our trip, and Rome was one of the last stops. We were staying in Garbatella, an architecturally rich, lesser-known neighborhood on the outskirts of the city center, a budding Brooklyn of sorts in that artists, families, and students found a respite from the city's din and cost in the winding streets lined with fascist-era apartment buildings and cypress trees straight out of a Dr. Seuss book. We knew little of the neighborhood apart from the fact that it was close enough to the city to be convenient but far enough away to have far cheaper prices.

We took the metro from the airport, dodging the smiling advances of ill-intended schemers, and I safeguarded our backpacks like a mama bird watching over her nest. When the train doors opened at the Garbatella station, we exited onto the heat of the platform with no real idea as to where we were. After checking our map, we set off. At this point in our journey, we had completely abandoned our commitment to light and nimble packs. With our return home imminent, we had begun accumulating all sorts of unnecessary things to bring back with us. It all started with a few trinkets from Germany—kitchen knives, jazz and pop records from a yard sale, and a set of miniature Riesling tasting glasses—and ended in total ridiculousness. We now carried with us a set of five copper pots, a "must have" Le Creuset soup pot we had found for €1 at a French flea market, four ceramic cups, an olive dish, a set of four ramekins, and a full case of Piemonte wine. These additions to our load resulted in David carrying more than seventy-five pounds on his back as well as a fifty-pound duffel and me carrying a fifty-pound pack and our travel guitar. Sweating, exhausted, and miserable, we slowly made the nearly two-mile walk to our accommodations. Things didn't improve when we arrived at our destination only to find our host wouldn't be home for another thirty minutes. Unsure if we had the stamina to carry our stuff much farther, we scanned the quiet residential street for some respite from the afternoon heat. A pretty shabby-looking coffee shop down the road seemed to be the only option. David's mood was spiraling into the treacherous realm of "hangry," and my sticky clothes were beginning to suffocate me.

The coffee shop didn't seem to have much in the way of anything we wanted. A slow oscillating fan was the only escape from the heat, but it was sadly behind the counter. The food selection was grim: uninviting sandwiches imprisoned in plastic wrap sulked behind smudged glass, and bags of potato chips collected dust on a spinning rack. There were few people in the shop apart from those who appeared to work there. The middle-aged woman behind the counter leaned against the bar, absentmindedly wiping down the espresso machine as she chatted with a man drinking a coffee and smoking a cigarette. In the back were some seedy-looking gambling machines manned by another smoking gentleman. Dropping our bags in the corner, we stretched our backs with a sense of relief and took a seat at one of the small tables outside. Pulling a cigarette out of who knows where, David went up to the counter, lit up with the rest of them, ordered coffee, and begrudgingly selected a sandwich from the case. Nothing disheartened David more than subpar food, especially in Italy.

We sat and chatted over our coffees. I took a puff of his cigarette, and we tried to rally a bit but with little success. Our coffees were brought over by the man behind the gambling counter, who interrupted our conversation. In clear English he asked, "Are you from America?" We nodded our heads and said, "Yes, coming from San Francisco." "Huh!" he said with a chuckle and went on to tell us how he drove a bus in Oakland for nearly twenty years and had only

recently returned to Rome. His name was Claudio. After some pleasant conversation, we asked if he knew of a nice place where we could get dinner. "If you want a good meal," he replied in that conspiratorial tone locals embrace when divulging a beloved secret to a new acquaintance, "you go to Paolo's. I can call him now and tell him you'll be coming tonight." With those simple words, our moods instantly lifted. We had the promise of a good meal endorsed by a local. Things were looking up.

That evening we followed Claudio's hand-drawn map to Paolo's restaurant. As we rounded the bend and first laid eyes on its lacquered striped awning and glaring fluorescent lighting, we hesitated for a moment before crossing the threshold. It was a Tuesday night, so the restaurant was fairly quiet. A lone disheveled waiter was bringing a carafe of red wine to one of the tables, and I launched into my practiced Italian greeting, telling him we were friends of Claudio's and that Paolo should be expecting us. He nodded at the mention of Claudio and seated us. *We felt surprisingly nervous, glancing sheepishly at our surroundings while trying to look natural.* We were clearly outsiders. The waiter returned with two menus, and I scanned mine to find something a celiac like myself could eat. Sadly, the menu was pasta heavy, and the only options that seemed safe were a side of sautéed chicory and possibly a meatball. *I guess I'll be hungry and frustrated in Rome*, I thought. When the waiter returned, I told him I had celiac disease, and he surprised me when, unfazed, he responded, *"Si, abbiamo pasta senza glutine."* (Yes, we have gluten-free pasta.) My cheeks flushed with excitement, and I could not hold back my emotion as I sat there grinning at the waiter. His face revealed a touch of pride, and we were off to a good start. David and I both ordered pasta all'Amatriciana, a signature Roman dish featuring a rich and lightly spicy tomato sauce riddled with crispy nuggets of bacon, and a one-liter carafe of the house red. When our pasta arrived, I felt like the waiter had bestowed a gift upon me. I had yet to order pasta in a restaurant in Italy, and as I took my first bite, I was awash with pure bliss. The pasta was perfectly al dente, and the sauce was decadent yet fresh, each ingredient singing to one another in harmony. I could taste the brightness of the olive oil, the sweetness of the tomatoes, and the savory bite of the bacon. I looked at David, and whether it was the shattering deliciousness of the meal, the three juice glasses of wine I had already drunk, or the seductiveness of the soft evening heat, tears stung the backs of my eyes. When the waiter asked if everything was good, I looked at him with pure joy. ***This is the best pasta* senza glutine *I have ever eaten," I said. He beamed.***

A moment later a man we presumed to be Paolo emerged from the back of the restaurant. He was stout and sturdy and looked like he might have killed a man or two. He came over to our table, evaluated us, and declared, "You are the friends of Claudio." We nodded our heads and complimented the food. He nodded again, but this time he revealed a surprising glimpse of tenderness from behind the scruff. We finished our meal, the entire liter of wine, and accidentally left a 50 percent tip. It was bliss.

We spent the next three days exploring the city, eating well, drinking cheaply, and walking through neighborhoods that danced the line between charming and derelict. Even though David had spent years building up this time in Rome, he did not experience an ounce of disappointment. He was completely enamored and engaged, and his excitement was contagious. Through his awestruck eyes, I saw a city I had known before in an entirely new light. Loud chaotic traffic became a beautiful tangle brimming with characters, as scooters, motorcycles, and small cars aggressively danced with each other. Less-than-savory characters became extra color, and dilapidated buildings became necessary contrasts to ancient masterpieces. Never missing *aperitivo* (happy hour with free snacks) and rarely spending any time in our apartment, we were charmed by Rome.

On our second afternoon in the city, we got a message from David's parents about attending mass at Saint Peter's Basilica. The service was to be about love, a topic they considered fitting for us. We thought we would enjoy it as a cultural experience, so we set off for the Vatican. I'm not sure if David had ever even seen a photo of the basilica before, because the minute he got a glimpse of the striking structure, he literally yelled "What?!?!" and ran into the middle of a heavily trafficked bridge to get a better view. Eventually making our way closer, we were stunned again, but this time by the gargantuan line of tourists snaking toward the entrance. Realizing that thinking we could make it in for mass was totally naive, I accepted defeat. David preserved his optimism and said, "Look at the priests. They're all walking quickly in the opposite direction of the line. I bet we could get one of them to take us in! Will you ask?" Aligning ourselves in their path, we let one priest go by, as he looked a bit less than friendly, but then David nudged me and said, "What about that one?" gesturing at an older priest making his way toward us. Something about the man seemed kind. Without hesitation, I approached him, and in broken Italian, asked whether the line in front of the basilica was indeed for mass. He explained the line was simply for people wanting to go into the basilica, mass or no mass, but when he saw our defeated expressions, he perked up and asked, "Do you really want to go to the mass?" We nodded our heads "yes," and he gestured with his hand and said, *"Avanti, avanti."* (Let's go.) **Without question, we followed him, weaving our way through the crowds of tourists.** He kept up a surprisingly quick pace, and we stayed close, repeatedly glancing at each other with huge stunned eyes. At first it seemed we were making a beeline for the basilica, but then our priest made a sharp turn left away from the crowds. In under a minute we found ourselves in front of a quiet side entrance, where two young Vatican guards dressed in colorful and traditional uniforms were waiting to check Vatican City passports. We had not known these existed!

The priest showed his passport and told the guards, "They're with me." The guards nodded, and we were let into what felt like another world: silent, pristine, and holy. After we made our first turn, the priest stopped and with a very subtle hint of excitement, waved his arm around the space, saying *"Niente, niente."* (Nothing, nothing.) Standing still for only a moment, I could hear only my own breathing from the pace we had been keeping. All around us was white and clean. I was instantly consumed with a feeling of peace and could not deny we were somewhere sacred. ***The priest then gave us a look I will never forget. It seemed to say, "I am proud to give you this gift."***

Within moments of stopping, the priest was rushing again, and we followed him through a back entrance into the sacristy. Everything was a blur as we passed through several rooms and even more guards. Suddenly, the priest opened an unassuming door, and we were in the center of Saint Peter's Basilica. The beauty was astounding and overwhelming. David was so overcome he had a hard time keeping up and quickly fell behind. The priest led us through the crowds, and I looked back to see David trying to overtake the gap by taking bigger, faster steps. The priest had a quick conversation with a guard, who lifted a large wooden barrier separating the mass area from where the public could freely walk, and the priest escorted us through the opening. He briefly shook our hands, and with a nod and a wink, bid us farewell. We never even learned his name.

There we were, attending mass at the Vatican with a group of roughly sixty people. As we took our seats and looked up at the pulpit, we realized we were in the presence of the Pope himself. The actual Pope was in front of us! It did not seem possible then, and when we think back on that day, it still doesn't seem real. The Pope spoke enthusiastically with a gentle yet undeniable authority. We were in awe and could not stop looking around us. Squeezing each other's hands, we were both overwhelmed by the experience and our great sense of partnership together.

MAKING YOUR WAY HOME

We didn't cope with our imminent homecoming by ignoring it; rather, we acknowledged its approach and made a mutual decision not to focus on it. The fact that we had saved one of our most desired destinations, Italy, for last also helped with our ability to stay in the moment and not get tangled up in all the logistics and worries going back home could have presented. Those last few weeks were some of the sweetest, and we savored each day as deeply as we could.

For us, there was a sense of exhilaration, a renewed energy to our rhythm, which emerged the closer to our return flight we got. Each day started to feel like the last because, in a way, it was. Before too long, we suddenly realized we had one week to go . . . ONE WEEK TO GO. Even though we had been gone for nearly a year, we would look at each other in wonder and ask, "Where did the time go?" Those last few weeks were truly the sunset of our trip, as golden in the moment as they are in our memories. It was a special time worth savoring.

CHAPTER 9

Adjusting to Reverse Culture Shock

Based on our own experiences and those of other travelers we know, some level of reverse culture shock is almost unavoidable after being gone for an extended period of time. Perhaps it was our academic and professional backgrounds in studying people, or memories of feeling unsettled upon coming home after a semester abroad in college, but we often found ourselves listening attentively to people's reentry stories. We heard tales across the spectrum, from very minor bumps in the road home to stories of significant struggle as people felt like foreigners in their own cities and towns.

Your homecoming could be simple or it could be difficult and lonely. For everyone else we know who traveled extensively, returning home was a surreal experience and more jarring than leaving had been. In this chapter, we share our experiences of coming home so that they can help you consider what home-coming may be like for you. We also provide some tips from experiences we had after returning home, as well as tips from other people we met on our travels, in hopes of helping you prepare for and manage any potential culture shock you may encounter.

Do You Have Exact Change?

New York City

DAVID

40.7128° N, 74.0060° W

Alexandra and I woke up heavy on our first day back in the U.S. Exchanging a few words, we went into the dining room of her grandmother's apartment in Manhattan to say good morning. Quickly the conversation moved from "How did you sleep?" to the family news before nestling into some less-than-pleasant health-related changes she had endured since our departure. Our trip did not come up, which was just as well, as my mood would have caused any story to fall flat.

Coffee! We need coffee. The realization snuck up on me like a flash and brought with it the hope that I had found the source of the dark cloud. Wanting to leave immediately for the closest coffee bar, but also wanting to be polite, I committed to another hour, which served to be unwise. After coming from Italy, where coffee is sold for a Euro on practically every corner, I was surprised how far we needed to walk to find an espresso. I expected to stumble upon a cool new-wave coffee bar, but a French-inspired chain store was the only thing within walking distance. As Google maps guided us through the Upper East Side, I was irritated both by everything around me as well as with myself for being so irritable. *What is wrong with you today? Time to get over whatever this is and enjoy a lovely sunny fall day in New York,* I thought to myself. Despite my best efforts, the vicious cycle continued; the cleanliness of our surroundings felt stuck-up, faces lacked depth, and everything felt superficial. *I was officially miserable.*

When we got to the coffee shop, I put on a chipper face, and we ordered two macchiatos as we had done every day for the last month in Italy. From behind the counter, a mildly confused face looked back at me with a disinterested smile and said, "What do you mean? Like a caramel one?" Still having the reflex to talk with my hands to overcome a language barrier, I signed out the beverage I meant to order while narrating with an apologetic tone. "Just a shot of espresso and a little bit of frothed milk in a tiny little cup about yea big," I said, holding space between my thumb and index finger. Seeming to understand, she inquired about any other purchases we would like to make and then stated the total, "That will be $5.01." I handed her $10.00, and she returned $4.99 to me in change.

Ninety-nine cents is a burden, I thought to myself. It is a weighty collection of nearly worthless metal that will sag my pockets until gone. Its only real value is its ability to help me not receive even more change throughout the day. It is also an emotional burden, a ploy for a forced gift. Rather than a tip above and beyond what is expected based on some sort of relationship or appreciated service, this feels like

I should thank her for removing this unwanted weight. My mind continued until I got to the heart of the issue; some money-grubbing owner who underpays his or her employees was forcing us to enter into these socially acceptable bribe-like scenarios where customers must choose between the guilt of not giving an obligatory gift or bear the bulging shameful weight in their pockets or purses. *What kind of country is this?* I ask myself. *This is a ridiculous system.* I imagined distributing my pennies and dimes and quarters to the customers in line before they found themselves trapped in the same miserable situation and then declare that we should no longer subsidize the owner's parsimony. The fantasy ended. I dropped the change in a jar and waited for my name to be called.

I would not say I am the type that meets change with grace. It is an uncomfortable and stiff set of clothing that requires a lot of effort to soften up. New York was always a place I dreamed about moving to when I was in my twenties. My sister had lived there for two decades, and the awe of the city never grew old no matter how many times I visited. How could a place of such beauty and wonder feel so dull and dingy now? Had I changed? Was the rest of the world so grand in comparison? Had the trip ruined one of the greatest cities in my home country for me?

After burning our tongues on the painfully hot watery beverage, we decided to get on the bus and go to the end of Central Park, then walk back. We boarded a bus on Fifth Avenue, and as we sat on our

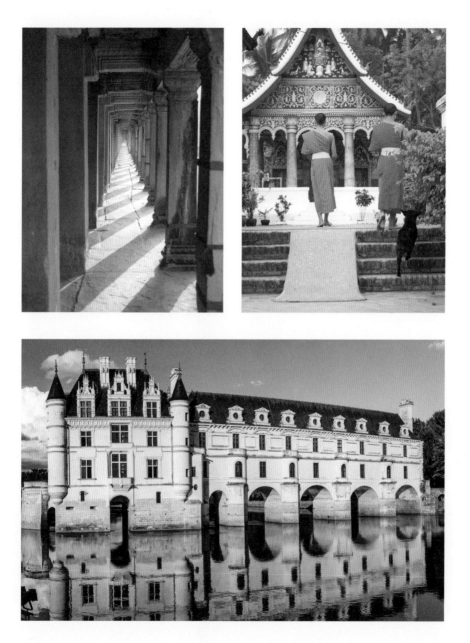

seats, the caffeine started to chase away a few clouds, and my thoughts were a bit less critical. I realized I needed to approach New York like I would any other destination on our trip. I needed to put aside my expectations, judgments, and comparisons and give it my best to see the place for what it was. Destinations are not scaled in any sort of linear fashion; they are at once beautiful and ugly, complex and simple. They are endlessly engaging, as they hold the history of the people and times before us while creating new ways to balance countless social, cultural, and physical dynamics every day. Of course, I love some places more than others for reasons within and beyond my understanding, but if I compared every new place to those I have loved before, I knew I would never have the chance to see and fall in love with where I was in the present moment. Sitting with this thought, I started to feel better.

After some silence, Alexandra and I started talking, and it seemed we were both going through similar fluctuations. One example led to another, and our comparably miserable experiences were becoming funny. The minute Alexandra described how alienating and out-of-body the entire morning had felt to her, I knew we were just in the throes of reverse culture shock and we would love this city again in no time. But in the meanwhile, we spared no detail as we went on and on about how dull and serious the people felt here, how commercial the environment seemed, how terrible and overpriced the coffee was, and so on. It felt good to just let it all out, so we did until I looked over Alexandra's shoulder to find an older gentleman having a bit less fun with our roasting of New York than we were. Realizing the obvious fact that most everyone in New York speaks English quite well, we both turned a bit red and rode the rest of the ride in silence.

Walking through the park that day, I realized my mood was not only a result of reverse culture shock but also a by-product of a good dose of ending-adventure sadness. I needed to update my résumé, find a job, and return to my more traditional day-to-day. I had no aspirations to travel for a lifetime, but I also had no interest in suiting back up and reentering the rat race. My stomach had felt sick for a month, which I had attributed to too much pizza and wine while in Italy, but now I recognized the feeling as a manifestation of my anxiety. ***While on the trip, I had not solved the problem of the mundane or thought of a way to be one of those people who loved a nine-to-five job.*** I had come up with a few business ideas, but starting a business can consume almost every moment of your waking life. I was not ready to sacrifice all the things I loved for a shot at loving my work.

What a lucky problem I have, I would tell myself as a reminder of the fantastic position I was in. *I have a great education, work experience, and network to fall back on.* Do not confuse life for fantasy. Not surprisingly, this kick-in-the-pants pep talk backfired, as it peppered guilt into my already bitter cocktail of anxiety. I needed to listen to myself and place a bet on me, not on the "follow the steady course" advice I had latched onto in my youth. That thinking might have gotten me this far, but it would take me back to where I started if I stuck with it. After making the difficult choice to quit my job and subsequently having the best year of my life, my motivation with decisions moving forward needed to be more genuine and rooted in something I sincerely cared about.

We had been walking through the park for a while, and I suddenly felt the strong urge to sit. I asked Alexandra if she would mind hanging out a bit by a small pond we were passing. We sat down on a nearby bench and watched as wooden remote-controlled sailboats drifted about on the water. I had always wanted to try sailing and was captivated by how simple and effective the concept was. With a slight breeze in the air, many of the boats seemed to be able to go wherever they wanted with finesse while others jerked about with little to no traction. Something about watching the boats made me feel better. *The adventure is not coming to an end,* I thought to myself. *It's just one adventure after the next.* Our trip was not a means to get back home; it was a means of experiencing life, places, and people like we had never done before. We were not trying to get anywhere and nor were we now. We were here to embrace the present, improve at the things we loved, build relationships, and live as much as we could every day. As we sat there in silence, I had a comforting thought: *in some ways, we are all like sailboats in a small lake, doing what we can with the wind given and hoping to give it a little finesse as we make our rounds.*

TIPS ON REENTRY

We found that in many ways it's easier to deal with places changing than you changing. It's jarring to be annoyed, bored, or plain disengaged with a place that was essentially your whole universe before you left. Cultural or societal practices that were once intuitive may feel strange and backward as you, perhaps unknowingly, adopted new ways of seeing the world during your time away. Unlike your mind-set when visiting somewhere new and exciting, preconceived assumptions and associations about home may also hold you back from engaging and therefore delay your acclimation process.

Additionally, you may find that your connection with some friends is a bit different than before you left. Although there is a chance you will ultimately find yourself gravitating to new people, we highly recommend not reading too much into feelings of disconnect in your first year back. Remember that you are most likely the one who has changed, and it's on you to be gracious and trust the connections you built before you left.

Reverse culture shock can be very unsettling, but there are ways to help cope with the transition. A few decisions we made for the first weeks back proved to be tremendously helpful in the long run and made our return home less jarring.

1/ Create a Plan for Coming Home

It can be tremendously helpful to have a general sense of how you want to approach coming home and set an intention around what you want to do, where you want your mind-set to

continued ⊷

be, and how you want to approach decisions. For example, here are a few questions to consider asking yourself before coming home:

- How quickly do you want to start searching for work?

- Do you want to make big changes or decisions right away?

- Do you want to live in the same place you were living before?

The answers to these questions will help you establish a plan for when you get back.

2/ Don't Take Reverse Culture Shock Too Seriously

You may feel pretty rough when you first get back, but it's important to remember that all the uncomfortable things you're thinking, feeling, and experiencing are a result of reverse culture shock. Just like mood swings or hormonal shifts or even getting the flu, this too shall pass. From what we gathered from other travelers we met, a common piece of advice was to not take negative feelings about home too seriously and to try to minimize judgment, knowing that you may be experiencing everything under the veil of difficult emotions caused by reentry, not the people and things around you. Also avoid making big life decisions or alienating friends you were once close with. Make note of how you're feeling but don't indulge in the feelings too deeply.

3/ Wean Yourself Off Travel

One of the best decisions we made was to come home but not go *home* to San Francisco right away. Instead, we slowly made our way back to the West Coast over three weeks. We visited family and friends in New York, Pittsburgh, Wisconsin, and Chicago, and even attended the Park City wedding of our round-the-world friends we had traveled with in New Zealand and Japan. Those three weeks of transition time were beyond beneficial for our adjustment period because even though we had "returned," we still felt like we were on the road. Being back in our apartment in San Francisco was surreal enough after three weeks traveling across the country, so we couldn't imagine how strange it would have been had we gone directly home and slept in our own bed on the first night back after nearly a year away.

4/ Create Bookends

A week into our trip around the world, we went to David's grandpa's house in northern Wisconsin, and a week before going back to our apartment in San Francisco at the end of our trip, we did the same. Having these bookends was very grounding. It helped us cement our intentions for the trip before leaving and gave us time for contemplation upon our return. Spending time in the same peaceful and comforting place at both the beginning and end of your trip can be really helpful in setting you up for not only a good journey but also a good homecoming.

continued ➛

5/ See Supportive People

This may seem a bit obvious, but you could run into a situation where some of the people closest to you or those you happen to see the most may not be keenly interested in hearing about your trip when you get back. You'll be eager to share the experiences you've just had with the people you care about, so try to surround yourself with the folks who are just as eager to hear about them. Not surprisingly, it feels much better to share stories with people who are genuinely interested.

6/ Cultivate a Sense of Self-Awareness

As tempting as it may be to compare things you're doing back home with similar situations on the road, keep in mind that people generally don't appreciate a comparative experience. For example, if you're eating at an Italian restaurant with friends, and someone compliments the food, reconsider before saying, "This is good, but it's not really how they make it in Italy." It doesn't take much to turn people off, as there's a fine line between sharing and undermining. Be sure to see where you are and be sensitive to those around you.

The Last Flight

San Francisco, CA

ALEXANDRA

37.7749° N, 122.4194° W

The sun had just made its final descent behind the horizon line as our plane touched the ground. The rear wheels screeched on the asphalt runway before the front touched down, and the air whooshed around the wings as the flaps flared up like preening peacocks on display. After nearly a year on the road, we were back in California, back to where it had all begun. I held David's hand, and he squeezed mine gently. We both turned our heads to look out the window at the lights on the runway and the dark hills rolling in the distance. We were home.

How many flights had we taken in the last year? How many times had we snugly secured our packs to make them look as small as possible and nestled them into the overhead compartment? How many different types of beverages were offered, and how many varied types of airplane meals gingerly wrapped in foil caps with plastic bottoms had we consumed? How many languages had we heard the safety information in? Transit had become as much a part of the fabric of our lives as the travel it facilitated, and the thought that we wouldn't have another flight coming up any time soon was disorienting. *At its core, the path ahead felt so clear: we would move back into our same apartment, start working again, and continue our life together.* But wrapping my head around how things would ultimately unfold felt nearly impossible. So much had happened in the last year. Our time away had been richer and denser than any other period in either of our lives, and each day had been ours alone. Apart from one day in Thailand, we had been together twenty-four hours a day, seven days a week, the entire time we had been on the road. I had a hard time imagining going back to a routine in which I didn't experience everything in lockstep with David. As we continued our amble down the runway, I held David's hand tighter.

"Here we are," I said.

"Here we are," he replied. Neither of us had to say anything more to understand we were feeling the same way.

The plane pulled into the gate, and the ding of the release signal unleashed the flurry of activity that always happens at the end of a flight. People eagerly sprang from their seats, gathering belongings and lining up to get off the plane. We didn't share in the sense of urgency around us. Part of me wanted to stay on the plane and continue onward. The line began to move, and before too long, it was our turn to stand, get our backpacks, and leave the plane. For most people, this was just another flight, another normal day in the routine of life, but for us, this flight was the end of a remarkable chapter.

David's sister and her wife were picking us up at the airport, and we were going to get Ethiopian food together on the way home. It was surreal to be back in the world of regular plans and coordinating schedules. We walked through the terminal, and the weight of my pack on my back was oddly comforting. I wanted to remember everything, even the way the carpeted floor of the terminal felt under my feet. Now that we were back, I couldn't believe I had thought I was ready to come home at some points during our trip.

We followed the signs for baggage claim and arrivals, and as we descended on the escalator, we saw David's sister and her wife waiting for us, large smiles spreading on their faces once they picked us out among the crowd. Seeing them again, I felt suspended in time. It was as if we had just said goodbye, but also as if we had not seen them for years. *It will be this way with everything,* I thought. Time had gone quickly, and time had gone slowly. What mattered was that we had had that time, and we would have this time now. This was the next chapter, the next adventure upon which we would embark together, and just as we hadn't known what the trip would be like, we equally didn't know what this next phase would bring. Maybe in a way we were still traveling after all.

ARE WE THERE YET?

David

Anticipating some bumps as we landed back into our life in San Francisco, we committed to not making any major decisions for at least six months. This served to be a good choice because within days of being back, Alexandra expressed a lack of enthusiasm for the city. The ballooning tech scene grated on her, the rampant homeless encampments were depressing, and the very high cost of living made rooting seem impossible. I was also disappointed with how the city, especially my neighborhood, had changed while we were away. This movement had been well on its way when we left, but taking a year off made its rapid pace that much more obvious. I felt the tech industry had priced out the soul of the city. San Francisco had gone from a city that, to me, embodied America's open frontier, where I would meet someone doing something wild and different almost every day, to a homogenous tech bubble filled with rich kids chasing fleeting trends. So many of the things I thought I loved about home seemed to be lost in the past. Luckily, most of the people we knew felt very similarly about what was happening, which helped us get over the shock and make sense of what was changing faster: us or home.

The shock of returning did eventually wear off after about six months. Although our observations and feelings toward the things that turned us off remained, we were able to engage with the city in a new way and start to envision a sustainable life here again. We were a part of the city again. Accepting the negatives and becoming accustomed to the cultural norms, we were able to more clearly see the larger picture and all the incredible parts of the city that still remained. That's not to say we didn't still question moving from time to time, and almost did at one point, but as time went on, we no longer felt like outsiders. We were home—happy and enjoying our life in San Francisco once again.

CHAPTER 10

Finding a New Perspective on Your Old Life

📷

This perspective is valuable. We found ourselves repeating this line often as we made the adjustment to being back home. We both felt a lot of pressure to slip right back into "normal life" and have the trip fade away. The pressures of home remained: career advancement, buying a home, buying a nicer home, having kids . . . the list went on. All these things were important to us, but we didn't want them to become all-encompassing. The trip pulled into perspective our values and all the elements of life that made the day-to-day feel rich. We had never been so in touch with the things that gave us joy, and we wanted to be conscious of how we approached reentry so that we didn't abandon what we had gained during our time away. When we would feel overwhelmed by making life work back home, and during the times when it all felt a bit impossible, we would remind each other that directing our energy into making a life that aligned with our values would be well worth it. We began to be able to see the tension and frustration we sometimes felt as helpful guides aiding us forward as we tried to be thoughtful with our choices.

Travel had a different effect on everyone we met, but a few things proved to be universal. After traveling for an extended period of time, you'll have gained a global perspective on issues, a deeper respect and love for our planet, the knowledge that most people in the world are good people, and an appreciation for a few new favorite foods. It's also highly unlikely that the trip will not affect your life back home in a significant way, even if your life looks a lot like it did before you left.

As with all the topics in this book, we hope to help you envision what it may be like for you to experience your reentry through our own story, to see your life from the perspective of the you that left, gained a mountain of experiences, and came back changed. In this chapter, we'll share our experiences of finding and building new paths and new lives at home by holding on to what we could from our year of travel.

How Over What

San Francisco, CA

DAVID

37.7749° N, 122.4194° W

"Could you have done this before?" a coworker asked. I began replying before my brain caught up, and I found myself rambling about an unknown, with no clear idea on how to address her question. I was not particularly impressed with what I was doing, so her question seemed a bit odd to me. I had a half-thought: *Do what? Consult? Of course; anyone in this field can.* But the other half was out of reach. I felt blindsided by an unexpected blend of emotions, like when I randomly want to have a full-on cry at a romantic comedy.

Scrambling to slow down my circling, I quickly chose a side. "No, I guess not," I said. In an attempt to understand why I was so taken by the question, I elaborated. "I guess I always envied consultants in my past because they made more, worked less, and had greater flexibility. I most likely would not have done it before, though, because it sort of puts your career on hold. I was terrified to do that then." While speaking, I wondered if she could tell how oddly large an impact her question had had on me.

As we stayed on the topic longer, I felt compelled to reveal a bit more about why I wasn't too impressed with myself for consulting.

"I thought I would come back and do something totally different," I said. "I wanted to build something I believed in, something I could pour my heart into. When I first started working in the corporate environment, it was such a miserable adjustment, and, honestly, I never expected to return to this office building. I think the me that left on the trip would see my current choice as a failure."

I didn't know this coworker well, but I could sense her adventurous spirit, and something about her made me think she saw success differently than many of my other coworkers did. This assumption proved to be accurate as she told me of her unique upbringing abroad and her exciting future ambitions to be CEO of a cause-oriented retail company. Somewhere in our conversation she mentioned the guts it took for me to quit and continue to address life on my own terms as a consultant. She went further and expressed how she would be far too scared to do the same. I felt a bit taken aback by this reveal; I was not surprised that she would be nervous to pause her hard-earned career and her life with a kid and a husband to travel around the world, but the way she felt about my current decision was perplexing.

All of a sudden, my mind was racing again with connections. *I am literally back working for my old boss in the same office building, yet I am in no way back to where I was before. I left something constrictive for something liberating: a job that kept me from what I loved for a job that enables me to do what I love, from feeling owned to feeling free,* *from a rat race to having fun, and from always sensing that I need to conform to feeling valued. **Stepping off my career path to travel has changed me.***

As I walked back to my desk, I realized that I didn't follow my plan to start a business because I didn't want to right now. It did not align with what I valued in this moment. I wanted time to do a variety of things, and this current role facilitated that. I also liked the daily challenge and felt lucky to have the opportunity to get paid for doing something that after years of work now came naturally. And I knew if that changed, I would figure out how to walk away and start something new.

Same Same but Different

San Francisco, CA

ALEXANDRA

37.7749° N, 122.4194° W

I stared at the computer screen, my eyes registering but not reading the rows of emails neatly stacked in my inbox. I had an inbox again. And a work email address. And tasks that were somehow overdue even though it was my first day on the job. *Focus,* I thought. You know how to do this. Just focus. But my mind bucked the instruction and continued to reel. I glanced up from my laptop at the people around me. These were my new coworkers. They were all seated around one gigantic table as part of the "collaborative and open work plan" the agency had adopted, like so many other companies had over the last few years. Some people had on headphones to block out noise while others chatted with their neighbors. Two guys were tossing a minia-ture basketball back and forth across the table as they talked about a project. **What have I done?** *I thought.* I had no idea how I was going to connect to these other people, let alone to the work I had been hired to do, at least not in the state of mind I was in right now.

Since I had gone back to the line of brand-strategy work I had done before, I thought the transition from traveling life to working life would be a bit smoother, but something about everything being so familiar yet seeming so off left me feeling isolated and depleted.

I couldn't seem to shrug away the voice in my head that kept whispering about how I had made a mistake. I wondered if the people around me could tell I was having a small existential crisis. I thought about texting David an SOS message but stopped myself. I got up from my seat and went to the kitchen to get a cup of coffee, hoping to discover my rallying spirit among the creamers, sugar packets, and stirrers. Going back to my seat, I took a deep breath and returned my attention to my inbox. *Just take it one email at a time,* I thought.

I got through that first day back at work, and as time went on, I began to adjust. I realized the year away hadn't made me any less competent at my job. Rather, I was surprised to find it had improved the way I worked. I was more efficient, more decisive, and the variety of experiences I'd collected over the last year had given me a fresh perspective when it came to my day-to-day responsibilities. I began to embrace setting boundaries in the workplace—something I had struggled with in the past. I got to work each day just before nine and rarely stayed later than five thirty. I didn't check my email at night or on the weekends. The job was going well, and while I still wasn't completely clear on whether or not it was the right place for me long-term, I felt confident in my decision to give myself six months rather than impulsively quitting right away like I had wanted to do on the first day.

I ultimately didn't stay at that agency much longer than the six-month deadline I had set, but that first job back gave me the confidence to start making professional decisions for myself rather than for all the "should" expectations I had previously set. After realizing I could still do the work but simply didn't want to anymore, I ended up bidding farewell to the world of advertising agencies and making the jump to the client side, which felt like a step in the right direction. Along the way, I began having conversations with a publishing house in the area. I had dreamed of working in books since I was a small child, so when I was given an offer in their marketing department a year later, I couldn't believe the childhood aspiration I had held on to for so long might become a reality. As much as I wanted the job, the decision wasn't easy. Leaving corporate marketing for publishing involved some pretty significant risks. I would be taking a title demotion and massive pay cut. On an emotional side, I again faced external pressures pushing me to not step off the path I was on, as well as my internal guilt of feeling like less of a "contributor" and more reliant on David. I also had some fears about jumping into a whole new industry I knew very little about, but all these concerns couldn't stand up to the pull I felt to follow my heart. With David's enthusiastic support, I accepted the offer and made a major career transition.

Most people in my life were encouraging of my decision, but a few were very vocal in their disapproval of me. Turns out that doing what you want is not always appreciated by others. Important figures in my life seemed incredibly disappointed about the fact that I would be making less money and working with less upside potential. This stung. As excited as I was about my new job, I couldn't help but feel the weight of this disapproval. The first few weeks at the publishing house were good but also a struggle, and even though I tried not to let it happen, I got sucked into a spiral of stress and doubt.

A good friend finally said the words that shook me from my reverie: "Release people to feel what they are going to feel and do not hold on to your instincts to please and not disappoint. You are on your path, and they are on theirs." With a shock, I realized the feelings I had been experiencing about deciding to take this new job were similar to those I had felt when David and I decided to leave on our trip. The connection was so simple and obvious, but I had missed it during all those weeks of emotional churning. What's more, David had been the one in search of something different when it came to work, not me. I had never really doubted my profession, even when we were on the road, but the trip had given me a new perspective and made it harder for me to ignore myself. I felt a newfound appreciation for the trip and its lingering effects, *how the decision to go in the first place was now the spark to fuel so many other decisions to live life on my terms.* It's hard to say whether I would have made the same choices had I not gone on the trip, but something in the back of my mind says I probably wouldn't have. Regardless, every day I go to work is now a reminder of how the trip has lived on, even if I'm no longer on the road.

EMBRACE WHAT'S POSSIBLE

Looking back at our year of travel, it was clearly the best year of our lives so far. It was not the easiest year by far, nor the smoothest, but in many ways we made the biggest bets we had ever made by following our hearts. Even if we didn't really understand what that meant at the time we left, we learned what that meant every day on the road. We began to realize that the impossible or improbable are far less so if we put ourselves in the path of receiving them. Even more than the experiences and memories we amassed, we now see this new perspective as the most valuable part of our travels. Our year off proved to be the reset button we had been seeking for how we wanted to live. While we're no longer on the road, we're still holding tight to what made that year so magical and hope to always do so.

A lot of people have asked us what changed the most after we took our trip, and while there are many ways to answer that question, one change is the most clear of all: so many more things feel possible now.

250

EPILOGUE

When we got back from our trip, we were curious to see what our relationship would be like at home and what our dynamic together would be without the constant changes and excitement of travel. In some ways we were both a little nervous, as we had never had a "normal life" together. Luckily, Bill Murray was right; life on the road proved to be really good prep for life at home. After six months we got engaged, and we planned a wedding, celebrating our commitment to one another under the Golden Gate Bridge almost one year to the day after setting foot back in San Francisco.

When it came to going back to work, we were shocked by how well our travels were perceived by future employers. No one batted an eye at the way we explained our sabbatical, and while we had initially feared the yearlong gap would translate to a dark spot on our résumés, it proved to be surprisingly bright, often sparking really interesting conversations and connections. The most common response we got was "I would love to do that." At the end of the day, people just got it.

Two and a half years have passed since we returned from our big trip. While not on the same scale, our travels have continued in that time. We scratch the itch by going away for two-week stretches, picking a new country we've never been to or focusing on a few local spots to visit. We still use our same backpacks and even took them on our honeymoon. We both get a kick out of how quickly we fall back into our patterns from life on the road, efficiently packing everything into the small spaces available to us while still managing to squeeze in a few indulgences here or there . . . bottles of wine, cool ceramics from little markets, leather shoes, and small things to remind us of the expansiveness of the world while we live our daily lives back home.

We still dream of traveling the way we did on our trip, of taking another long adventure to all the places we did not have time to explore the first time around, but new adventures await us here at home. The biggest may be that we are expecting our first child—a fact we learned of a month after committing to write this book. We have no idea what new changes this addition will bring, but we are already considering what to do with our maternity and paternity leaves. Maybe back to France, or perhaps somewhere warm. . . .

Travel and traveling together have left such a positive impact in our lives that we often find ourselves encouraging people who show interest in taking the leap. This is a big reason we wanted to write the book. Travel awakened a part of ourselves that helps us remain engaged in our lives. We still fall into all the challenges home life can bring and the temptation to put our heads down and plow through, but after the trip, it's harder to ignore what we care about in lieu of what's expected. The trip also really reinforced in us the belief that there is no sustainable option to be anything or anybody other than yourself. In this way, it has yet to end; rather, taking a year off was just the beginning.

253

ACKNOWLEDGMENTS

This book has been a labor of love from the start. We feel so lucky to have had this opportunity and are endlessly grateful to those who helped us along the way.

First and foremost, thank you to our team at Chronicle Books: Deanne Katz, Christine Carswell, Jennifer Tolo Pierce, Diane Levinson, Sarah Lin Go, Christina Loff, Marie Oishi, Freesia Blizard, and Meghan Legg. Thank you so much for creating a book we can be so proud of.

Thank you to Heather Kelly, Josh Haftel, John Zeratsky, Megan Sovern, Sonya Thomas, Daniel Schmidt, and Tenaya Middleton for helping us put a proposal together.

Thank you to Vaunda and Drew Nelson for helping turn a proposal into a book and to Alan Clarke, John and Nedra Roberts, and Arvand Khosravi for helping us through the process.

Thank you to RC Rivera and Josh Haftel for all things photography and Danielle Grey for design.

Thank you to our parents, Andrei and Laurie, Justin and Christyl, and our siblings and siblings-in-law, Hilary, Jarrett and Hallie, Tricia and Kerry, and our grandparents, Howard, Gayle, Francine, and Bob for supporting our collective capabilities, championing our dreams, and cheering us on along the way.

Thank you to Ali Shoule and Amber Cooper for giving the book its first test run.

Thank you to Marian Milut for your enduring blessing to us.

And to our daughter, Emma Cléo. You have opened our hearts in ways we couldn't have imagined. We cannot wait to show you all the wonderful things to see in this great wide world.

PHOTOGRAPHY

We took all the photos in this book with an inexpensive, light, and compact mirrorless camera and a fixed 50mm f/2.0 "pancake" lens. The final photos you see were edited with Adobe Lightroom on our Macbook Air while we were still abroad. If you've wondered where exactly these images were taken, this index will point you to the location of each photo in the book.